# A TEMPLE FOR BYZANTIUM

Martin Harrison

# A TEMPLE FOR BYZANTIUM

## The Discovery and Excavation of Anicia Juliana's Palace-Church in Istanbul

WITH A FOREWORD BY SIR STEVEN RUNCIMAN

UNIVERSITY OF TEXAS PRESS, AUSTIN

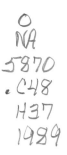
International Standard Book Number 0–292–78109–1
Library of Congress Catalog Card Number 89–50511

First University of Texas Press Edition, 1989

Originating Publisher HARVEY MILLER LTD · 20 Marryat Road · London SW19 5BD · England

# Contents

*Poem referring to St. Polyeuktos in the 'Anthologia Palatina' written in Constantinople (?)*
*in the tenth century. Heidelberg, University Library, Cod. Pal. Gr. Heid. 23, p. 50*

# Foreword

TO THE DELIGHT of romantically minded historians the Byzantine Empire produced in the course of its long history a number of great ladies whose careers affected its destiny. There were empresses such as Theodora, wife of Justinian, her namesake, wife of Theophilus, Irene the Athenian and Theophano the Spartan, scholar princesses such as Anna Comnena, or, of lesser importance, Casia the poetess, whose feminist pertness lost her the crown, and the Empress Euphrosyne, unrivalled mistress of corruption. But none was more formidable than the Lady Juliana Anicia, who lived from 462 to about 528. She was the greatest heiress of her time. Her father's family had been distinguished since the days of the Roman Republic. Her mother was descended from the daughter of Theodosius the Great and the daughter of Theodosius II. Her father Olybrius had been briefly Emperor of the West. Her husband, a distinguished general of Germanic origin, had been offered but refused the throne of the East when revolt seemed likely to depose the Emperor Anastasius. She had hoped that her son, a younger Olybrius, might succeed Anastasius, into whose family he had married. But instead the throne passed to a soldier of illiterate peasant background, Justin I: for whom and for whose nephew and heir, Justinian I, she felt profound and undisguised contempt. She was too formidable for them to restrain her; but Justinian must have sighed with relief when she died, in her middle sixties, in 528.

The times in which she lived are of great interest to art-historians, as they saw the first synthesis of the elements that made up Byzantine art, the Roman taste for solid splendour and for competent craftsmanship, the Greek sense of balance and proportion and enjoyment in mathematical experiment, and the oriental love of varied ornament and even fantasy, together with the need to create a setting suited to the rites of the Christian Empire and the Christian Church. It was in architecture that the new synthesis was most successful; but the history of its development is not easy to trace. There are no surviving buildings in Constantinople dating from the period between the building of the old-fashioned basilica of St. John Studion in the mid fifth century and the building of the great monuments of Justinian's reign, culminating in the incomparable cathedral of St. Sophia. Some information about the intermediate architecture was badly needed to fill the gap.

It was known from a long epigram that survived in the Palatine Anthology that the Lady Julia Anicia had seen to the building of a great church dedicated to her favourite saint, the soldier-martyr Polyeuktos. But where was it? The work of developers in our modern cities is usually deplorable; but occasionally it has its serendipity. In 1960 work on the foundations of the new City Hall of Istanbul brought to light part of an inscription on marble which was identified as being part of the epigram about Juliana Anicia's church. Four years later the preliminary stages of the construction of an underpass road brought bull-dozers to an open space nearby; and more pieces of marble were revealed. The Turkish archaeological department hastily intervened; and permission to work at the site was given to its own archaeologists, under the late Dr. Nezih Firatli, and the Dumbarton Oaks Institute of Washington, D.C., whose team was headed by an Englishman, Professor R. M. Harrison.

The account of the excavations that followed reads like an archaeological detective story. In six hard-working seasons the teams succeeded, by the meticulous and enterprising assemblage of evidence, in discovering not only the ground plan of this great building but also its probable elevation, and details of its remarkably rich decoration, fragments of which had travelled as far afield as Spain. We can now see the part that it played in the development of the splendid architecture of sixth-century Byzantium.

Perhaps the most fascinating outcome of the excavation was to reveal the inspiration that lay behind the building. The epigram that adorned its walls compared Juliana Anicia to Solomon whose temple hers surpassed. Detailed examination of the ground plan shows how exactly her architects copied the measurements of the great Temple in Jerusalem as it was described in Holy Writ. Solomon was the archetypal king in the Bible; and the Princess, conscious of her high lineage, was determined to erect a royal place of worship next to her palace, as an act of defiance against the upstart Emperors of her time. It is no wonder that the Emperor Justinian, when his architects completed the even vaster and more splendid church of St. Sophia, exclaimed with complacency 'Solomon, I have vanquished thee'. This formidable old lady was the Solomon that he had in mind.

We owe a great debt of gratitude to Professor Harrison for telling us the story of this remarkable archaeological achievement in terms that the laity can understand.

*Steven Runciman*

For Işın Fıratlı and Mary

The Author and Publishers wish to thank all those
who have contributed additional illustrations for this book,
in particular Professor C. Mango, Professor R. Mark,
Professor T.F. Mathews, and Ms Sheila Gibson
who provided the diagrams, elevations and reconstructions

# Preface

THE SITE of Anicia Juliana's palace-church of St. Polyeuktos was rediscovered in 1960, and excavation began four years later, lasting fifty-six weeks spread over six seasons. The full and detailed specialist report has been published separately in two large volumes, but the results are of such exceptional interest and importance, from architectural, artistic and historical points of view, that it seemed desirable to provide also a short selective account of the church itself unencumbered by too much archaeological detail. Early Byzantine archaeology is in its infancy, and it is hoped that this book, presenting material which throws entirely new light on the major formative period of Byzantine art, will be of interest both to the general reader and to students of art, architecture and archaeology.

The excavations were carried out by Dumbarton Oaks (Harvard University's centre for Byzantine studies) and the Istanbul Archaeological Museum, under the joint direction of the late Dr. Nezih Firatli and myself. Principal staff included Dr. Margaret Gill (small finds), Mrs. Elizabeth Harrison (photography), Dr. John Hayes (pottery), Mr. Gordon Lawson and Miss Ülkü Izmirligil (architects), Mr. Christopher Arthur, Dr. Nusin Asgari, Mr. Colin Burgess, Professor Barri Jones, Mr. John Little, Miss Penny Pfeiffer, Mr. Saamin Sismanoglu, Mr. John Tait and Mr. Michael Vickers (site-supervisors). After the end of the excavation, the coins were studied by Mr. Michael Hendy, the brick-stamps by Dr. Stephen Hill, and the animal-bones and molluscs by Professor Kurt Kosswig. Valuable support and technical and administrative help were provided at all stages by the Archaeological Museum. The labour-force rose from fifteen in the first season to sixty-seven in the fourth. Serif Çavus was the foreman, and the core, who were with us for all six seasons, included Ali Eryigit, Recep Çelik, and Sabahattin Yurtseven. A more hardworking and trustworthy team of workmen would be difficult to find. The cost of the six seasons, including fares from Britain, was approximately $96,000.

Particular thanks are due both to Mr. Necati Dolunay, then Director of the Istanbul Archaeological Museum, and to the late Mr. Hikmet Gürçay, Director-General of Antiquities. Amongst very many visitors to the site who gave valuable advice and help (and these were legion), special mention may be made of Professor Semavi Eyice, Miss Alison Frantz, Mr. Ernest Hawkins, and Professors Ernst Kitzinger, Richard Krautheimer, Cyril Mango, James Morganstern, Ihor Sevcenko, Lee Striker, and Paul Underwood.

Small finds, selected items of pottery, figured sculpture, animal bones, and the more elaborate marbles, have been deposited in the Istanbul Archaeological Museum. The majority of the excavated material has been kept on site, in a large storeroom which was constructed within the substructures of the church's north aisle. A detailed scheme for landscaping the site as an archaeological park, was drawn up by Mr. Ralph Griswold in 1968, and in 1969 accepted by the Istanbul municipal authorities. So far only the first part of the scheme has, however, been implemented.

After the excavation came a long period of collation and study, on site, in the Istanbul Archaeological Museum, and at Newcastle, where I was ably assisted in the preparation of the full report by Mrs. Lynn Ritchie. Interim reports had appeared annually in *Dumbarton Oaks Papers*; the full report, with detailed accounts of the structures and stratigraphy, and specialist studies of sculpture, revetment, mosaic, brick-stamps, small finds, coins, bones and molluscs, including a great deal of later Byzantine and Ottoman material, and a second volume on the pottery and glass by John Hayes, has been published by Dumbarton Oaks and the Princeton University Press. Both in the compilation of the full report and in the preparation of this brief synoptic account of the church, I have been greatly helped by my secretary, Mrs. Wendy Young. Finally, I should like to acknowledge the kindness of the Princeton University Press in allowing me to draw substantially on material in Chapters 2, 5 and 15 of the first volume of the full report, *Excavations at Saraçhane in Istanbul*.

*Institute of Archaeology and All Souls College,*
*Oxford, 1989*

# THE EXCAVATION AND DISCOVERY
## OF ST. POLYEUKTOS

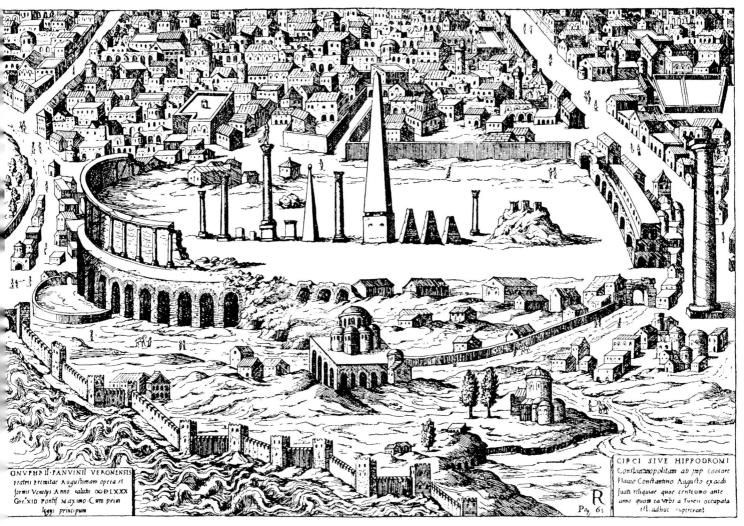

1. The ruins of the Hippodrome,
originally Roman but considerably
enlarged by Constantine and richly
adorned by his successors.
Engraving, 1450.

# I · Constantinople and Anicia Juliana

T HE ROMAN SOLDIER POLYEUKTOS was martyred for his Christian faith at Melitene (the modern town of Malatya in eastern Turkey) probably in the year 251. Until recently he was perhaps best known as the subject of a tragedy by Corneille and an opera by Gounod, but to these two artistic productions must now be added a third, the church dedicated to him by the princess Anicia Juliana in sixth-century Constantinople.

The site of the church of St. Polyeuktos, in the centre of the ancient city, was discovered by chance in 1960, and subsequent excavations gradually revealed the remains of a building of extra-ordinary splendour and importance. To appreciate this import-ance, however, we should, before we examine the church, look first at the geographical and historical background, and in particular at the growth and success of the city which succeeded Rome as Imperial capital.

Rome, situated a dozen miles up-river on the western side of Italy, was ill-placed to be the capital of an Empire which extended from the Tyne to the Tigris and from the Atlas to the Caucasus (see map on end-papers). In particular it was remote from its northern and eastern frontiers, which in the third century were under almost constant Barbarian or Persian threat and often overrun. To counter this, new Imperial capitals grew up at Trier and Milan in the West, and at Sirmium, Thessalonica and Nicomedia in the East. Rome itself became something of an anachronism (the Emperor Diocle-tian visited it for the first time in 303 to celebrate twenty years' rule), and there were thus precedents for Constantine in 324 when he settled on the small provincial city of Byzantium as the site of a new eastern capital, which was inaugurated in 330 and called Constantinople or New Rome.

The choice was inspired, in terms both of access and defence. At the southern end of the Bosphorus on the European side, it lay where east-west land-routes between Europe and Asia converged on the narrow crossing, and astride the north-south sea-lanes between the Black Sea and the Mediterranean. It was thus well placed to deal with problems both on the Danube and on the

≺ *2. General view of the foundations of St. Polyeuktos, from the west, across substructures north of the atrium. In the background, the Sehzade Mosque and a wing of the City Hall.*

Euphrates. The Golden Horn, a long deep-water inlet on its northern side, provided an incomparable harbour and served to define an easily defensible peninsula. Byzantium, which was colonized from Megara in the seventh century B.C., had become a Roman city largely rebuilt, after siege and destruction, in the first quarter of the third century. It lay at the tip of the peninsula and formed the nucleus of Constantine's very much larger city.

Although Constantine had promoted Christianity, his city, with its colonnaded streets, piazzas, monuments, and public and private buildings, was not at first conspicuously Christian. He himself was not baptised until he was on his deathbed in 337, and, although a handful of churches are attributed to him, the first cathedral of St. Sophia was not dedicated until 360, and the church of the Holy Apostles was originally constructed as his mausoleum. In 381, however, the Bishop of Constantinople was made pre-eminent above those of Alexandria and Antioch, and in 390 the Emperor Theodosius I closed all pagan temples and banned their cults.

With the construction of massive new land-walls in 413, Theodosius II virtually doubled the area of the city to enclose some 1,400 hectares (nearly eight square miles); and yet an inventory of the time lists only 14 churches, as against 14 palaces, 8 public and 153 private bath-houses, 5 granaries and 4,388 substantial houses.[1] The population at this period may have been as much as a quarter of a million. The principal surviving monuments of this period are the Hippodrome (fig.1), two triumphal arches (figs. 4, 5), various honorific columns (figs.6, 12) an aqueduct (fig.7), cisterns (fig.8), open reservoirs, the land-walls (fig.9), parts of three or four palaces (fig.10), and the remains of as many churches.[2] The church of St. Sophia, which had been burnt to the ground in 404, was rebuilt in 415, and fragments of the richly-carved outer gateway of this re-building have been uncovered by excavation (fig.11). Although so little remains, or has been brought to light, what we do have confirms the quality of the decoration and is consistent in the story it tells.

16

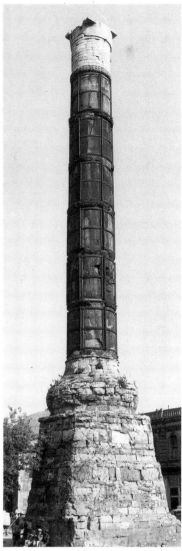

6. *Porphyry column erected by Constantine in his Forum. The column, which has been much repaired and consolidated, once carried the statue of Constantine and is the only major monument in the city surviving from Constantine's reign.*

5. *The Golden Gate, a triple arch, stood about one mile outside Constantine's walls on the Via Egnatia, the principal road to the west. It was incorporated into the new walls of Theodosius II in 413.*

17

7. *Aqueduct of Valens, begun by the Emperor Valens (364-78) probably in 368 and*
*carrying water from the hills north-east of the city to a central distribution-point in the Forum of Theodosius.*

8. *Cistern known as the 1001 Columns (Binbirdirek), one of two gigantic covered cisterns in the city.*
*The columns are placed one on top of another, and originally there were 224 such double columns.*

9. *The Land Walls constructed by Theodosius II in 413*
*approximately one mile outside the walls of Constantine.*

10. *Palace-apartments overlooking the Sea of Marmara and built on top of the city's Sea Walls.*
*The doorways originally opened on to balconies.*

Like any new capital city, Constantinople had to draw at first upon other older centres for its craftsmen, art, and ideas. First among these older centres were Alexandria and Antioch, as well as other great cities like Ephesus. In architecture and sculpture, Constantinople's transition from a conservative and dependent city to one that was creative and influential in its own right, seems not to have occurred before about 500, to judge from the little evidence we have. The second church of St. Sophia (415), that of St. John of Studios of about 450 (figs.13, 21), and St. Mary in Chalcoprateia (of about the same date), were all simple timber-roofed basilicas with nave, side-aisles, galleries, and narthex. Architectural sculpture, as exemplified by the Golden Gate (about 390), the outer gateway of St. Sophia (fig.11), St. John of Studios (fig.13), and the Column of Marcian of 450-452 (fig.12), exhibits traditional forms such as composite capitals and modillion cornices, mouldings (roundel, ovolo, cyma reversa), and motifs known as bead-and-reel, egg-and-dart, leaf-and-tongue, acanthus-scroll, and erect acanthus. The repertory is standard, and the carving for the most part perfunctory. The cruciform plan of Constantinople's church of the Holy Apostles, and the elaborate form and decoration of the Arch of Theodosius I at Beyazit, were exceptional.

*11. Entablature block from the gateway to Theodosius II's church of St. Sophia (415),*
*showing the use of bead-and-reel, egg-and-dart, leaf-and-tongue, and acanthus.*

12. *Capital of the Column of Marcian (450-452), near Saraçhane.*

13. *Capital and entablature of the church of St. John of Studios.*

Surviving monuments are few, and almost nothing is known archaeologically about Constantinople in the later fifth century and early sixth. But with the accession of the Emperor Justinian in 527 the situation changes dramatically.

In 532 the fifth-century church of St. Sophia was, like its predecessor, destroyed by fire. This time, however, there arose from the ashes not another timber-roofed basilica, but the huge brick-domed building which still stands today (figs.14, 15, 22). To design it Justinian commissioned Anthemius of Tralles and Isidorus of Miletus who were theoretical engineers rather than architects, and St. Sophia was dedicated just five years later, in 537. The dome, of brick, is approximately 32 metres in diameter, crowning the square central bay of the nave 30.95m at ground level (equivalent to one hundred Byzantine feet). To East and West are two great semi-domes, and lateral thrusts are countered by an elaborate series of piers, buttresses and vaults. The dome collapsed later in Justinian's

*14. Justinian's church of St. Sophia (532-37).*

reign, in 558, and was quickly replaced by the present dome, now some twenty feet higher.[3] The present dome, which was twice severely damaged in the Middle Ages but on each occasion repaired, is almost hemispherical. It rises from a circular cornice, which is supported by pendentives, and the likelihood is that the earlier, shallower dome also had pendentives. The sheer scale of the building and the elegance of the design are breathtaking, and St. Sophia is deservedly regarded as the greatest architectural achievement of Late Antiquity. In decoration, too, there are remarkable innovations. Basket-capitals, carved overall with horizontally splayed or vertical acanthus-leaves deeply etched and undercut (fig.15), now replace corinthian or composite capitals. The principal entablature has an overall acanthus-scroll, where natural or traditional forms are completely subordinated to design. This formality in decoration was to become the hallmark of Byzantine art.

*15. Capitals and entablature of the nave-colonnade in Justinian's church of St. Sophia. These basket capitals, overspun with acanthus, retain vestigial Ionic volutes.*

Until recently the only earlier comparable building was the much smaller and simpler church of Saints Sergius and Bacchus, erected by the Empress Theodora sometime between the years 527 and 536 (fig.17). Here the dome rises by what are in effect squinches over an octagonal bay set within a square. The solution is clumsier, and perhaps the most successful feature of the church is again the series of richly carved basket-capitals (fig.16). Another surviving church from Justinian's reign is St. Eirene (fig.18), a large vaulted basilica with a dome on pendentives above the eastern part of the nave. An important church which has not survived was his reconstruction of the Holy Apostles, of which we have a contemporary description by the historian Procopius and his statement that Justinian's church of St. John at Ephesus (the ruins of which do survive) was modelled on it.[4] The plan was cruciform, with one dome over the crossing, two over the length of the nave, and one over each of the other three arms.

*16. Capital and entablature of the church of Sts. Sergius and Bacchus. The basket-capital is in the new style, and the long inscription in relief is reminiscent of St. Polyeuktos, but in its details (bead-and-reel, egg-and-dart, acanthus-scroll) the entablature is very conservative.*

*17. The church of Sts. Sergius and Bacchus (between 527 and 536), from the south-west. Eight masonry piers, separated by open exedrae and the sanctuary, carry the dome, which thus rises from an octagonal base.*

*18. The church of St. Eirene (532 and 740).*

It is evident that domes became a regular feature of major Constantinopolitan churches, and the architecture of the capital could now influence that of the provinces. Moreover, domes could be set over oblong naves, thus combining in the building both great height and length.

The domed basilica, as exemplified by St. Sophia — a building on a gigantic scale designed, as we have seen, with singular elegance — appeared, till our own day, to have no antecedents in Constantinople. In the provinces, the first true pendentives, admittedly tiny in comparison with those in the capital, were recorded at the monastery of Abu Mina near Alexandria in the early fifth century.[5]

Later in that century we know of a group of four churches in Isauria in southern Asia Minor, each on a basilical plan having a central tower with squinches. The churches are at Alahan (the best preserved) (fig.19), Dag Pazari, Meryemlik, and Korykos; they were almost certainly built by the Emperor Zeno (474-491), a native of Isauria who is known to have constructed a church at Meryemlik.[6] Whether the squinches carried a light dome or, as several scholars have recently argued, a low pyramidal roof of timber, the combination of longitudinal plan and central vertical axis was evidently now firmly established. Belonging to the sixth century, and probably dating from its second quarter, is a recently discovered group of churches in Lycia, also in southern Asia Minor. These are characterized by a *triconchos* (trefoil) sanctuary with three apses, to north, east, and south, preceded by nave and side-aisles. The bay defined by the three apses is square, and, although

*19. The East Church of the monastery at Alahan (late fifth century), from the east. Note the central tower which rises above the east end of the nave.*

in three cases (those at Karabel, Devekuyusu and Dikmen) the sanctuary is in a ruinous state, in the fourth, at Alacahisar, it is rock-cut, and true pendentives and the lower part of the crowning dome are well preserved, in clear imitation of masonry (fig.20).[7] It is thought that Alacahisar was constructed as a replica of Karabel, to which it corresponds closely in dimensions and for which a strong case can be made that it was built in the 530s, i.e. about the same time as Justinian's St. Sophia. Interesting developments in both plan and elevation were thus taking place in the provinces in the late fifth and early sixth centuries. In the capital itself, it seems improbable that the architects Anthemius and Isidorus would have embarked upon a domed basilica of the scale and assurance of St. Sophia, unless there had been some relevant antecedents - and, as the traditional vaulting-material in Constantinople was

*20. Rock-cut triconchos church at Alacahisar in Lycia (sixth century, probably second quarter), looking towards the sanctuary from the west end of the south aisle. The sanctuary was carved in the living rock; the rest of the church was added in masonry which had fallen. Note the perfectly formed pendentive between the northern and eastern apses and the lower part of the dome.*

brick, whereas in the mountainous regions of Isauria and Lycia it was cut stone, it seemed likely that such antecedents would be local.[8]

A number of great churches associated with Justinian happen to have survived, as have the writings of the historian Procopius, whose description of Justinian's buildings, both in Constantinople and in the provinces, is something of a panegyric. In view of the paucity of securely-dated earlier remains, the tendency has probably been to attribute too much to Justinian. The architectural and sculptural novelty of St. Sophia (and indeed of Saints Sergius and Bacchus) has been enhanced by the fact that the last church to have been built in the capital which has survived, was St. John of Studios, three quarters of a century before (fig.21).

21. View of the church of St. John of Studios (c. 450), from the east. This was a timber-roofed basilica with nave, aisles, galleries, and a flat entablature above the nave colonnades.

22. Interior view of St. Sophia. The brick ➤ dome 100 feet in diameter is raised on four massive piers, arches which spring from them, and pendentives.

23. Raising a pier capital during the first digging campaign in 1964.

24. A group in our team: our three main diggers, Ali, Sabaetin and Recep.

25. The author working at the south-east corner of the nave in the first campaign in 1964.

26. *The axial passage beneath the nave floor during excavation, looking west. In the foreground is the curving passage around the ambo-foundation, then a line of marble-blocks as fallen (the nearest carries Line 9 of the entablature, then the palm-tree pier-capital, and thirdly two fragments of the entablature arch with Line 16). The figure in the upper left is standing on the solid packing for the nave floor; behind him, in section, is the white layer of marble- waste upon which the mosaic-floor was laid.*

27. *Excavation of the substructures of the north-western sector (Baptistery?). The walls are of brick, and the plaster was added in the twelfth century, when the substructures were converted into a cistern.*

28. *Recep cleaning masonry during the excavation.*

*29. General view of the excavations from the south-east, at the end of the fifth season (1968).*

In 1960 grading operations around Istanbul's new city-hall at Saraçhane in the centre of the ancient city, uncovered a number of marble blocks. Two of these carried part of an inscription in raised letters about 11 cm. high (fig.34). The surviving words were recognized by Ihor Sevcenko as coming from a poem of 76 hexameter lines whose text is preserved in its entirety in the *Palatine Anthology*, a collection of ancient verses and epigrams which was compiled in about the year 1000.[9] This particular poem is in praise of the Byzantine princess Anicia Juliana, her royal lineage, and the elaborate and sumptuous church which she erected in honour of St. Polyeuktos, that obscure military saint martyred at Melitene in Cappadocia probably in 251. Evidently his relics had been transferred to Constantinople in the early fifth century, for we learn from the poem that Anicia Juliana's church replaced a similar one which had been built on the site by the Empress Eudocia, the wife of Theodosius II. The relics would have included the skull of St. Polyeuktos, which is known from an eleventh century source to have been there in the medieval period. The growing movement of holy relics to Constantinople served to increase the attraction and importance of the capital. Anicia Juliana's choice of saint was probably determined, at least in part, by her wish to stress her imperial family connection with Eudocia.

The poem falls into two parts, the first praising Anicia Juliana and her royal descent, the second mainly describing the church. Both parts refer to her family past, present and future. The following extracts, in literal translation, may serve to give some idea of both content and style:

'The Empress Eudocia, in her eagerness to honour God, was the first to build a temple to the divinely inspired Polyeuktos; but she did not make it as fine or as large as this, not because of any restraint or lack of resources — for what can a Queen lack? — but because she had a divine premonition that her family and descendants would have the knowledge and resources to provide grander embellishment. From this stock Juliana, bright light of blessed parents, sharing their royal blood in the fourth generation, did not disappoint the hopes of that Queen, who was the mother of its finest children, but raised this building from its small original to its present size and form.' (lines 1-10)

'Following on all the well-founded footsteps of her parents, she gave birth to a family which is immortal, always treading the full path of piety. Wherefore may the servants of the heavenly King, to whomsoever she gave gifts and to whomsoever she built temples, protect her readily with her son and his daughters. And may the unutterable glory of the most industrious family survive as long as the Sun drives his fiery chariot.' (lines 34-41)

'What choir is sufficient to sing the work of Juliana, who, after Constantine - embellisher of his Rome, after the holy golden light of Theodosius, and after the royal descent of so many forebears, accomplished in few years a work worthy of her family, and more than worthy? She alone has conquered time and surpassed the wisdom of renowned Solomon, raising a temple to receive God, the richly wrought and graceful splendour of which the ages cannot celebrate. How it rises from deep-rooted foundations, springing up from below and pursuing the stars of heaven, and how too it is extended from east to west, glittering beyond description with the brightness of the sun on both sides! On either side of the central nave, columns standing upon sturdy columns support the rays of a golden roof. On both sides recesses hollowed out in arches have given birth to the ever-revolving light of the moon. The walls, opposite each other, have recalled to life in measureless paths marvellous meadows of precious materials, whose brightness nature, flowering in the deep depths of the rock, has concealed and guarded for the house of God, to be the gift of Juliana.' (lines 42-64)

'Such is the labour that Juliana, after a countless swarm of labours, accomplished for the souls of her parents, and for her own life, and for the lives of those who are to come and those who already are.' (lines 74-76)

The first forty-one lines of the poem were carved around the nave of the church, according to marginal notes in the manuscript, and the remainder were to be found in the narthex and courtyard. Moreover, the notes state, the church had taken just three years to build. Furthermore, a tenth-century source, the *Book of Ceremonies*, relates that the Church of St. Polyeuktos lay on a processional route from the Forum of Theodosius to the Church of the Holy Apostles: '... and, following the Mesê, he (the Emperor) proceeds by way of the Bakers' quarter and the Forum Tauri (i.e., the Forum of Theodosius). Reaching the church of the all-holy Mother of God of the Diaconissa, the Emperor hands over the processional candle, and, crossing the Philadelphion, he veers to the right and comes by way of the quarters of Olybrius and of Constantiniana to St. Polyeuktos. Changing his candle there, and taking another from the praepositus (an official), he continues along the Mesê to the Holy Apostles.'

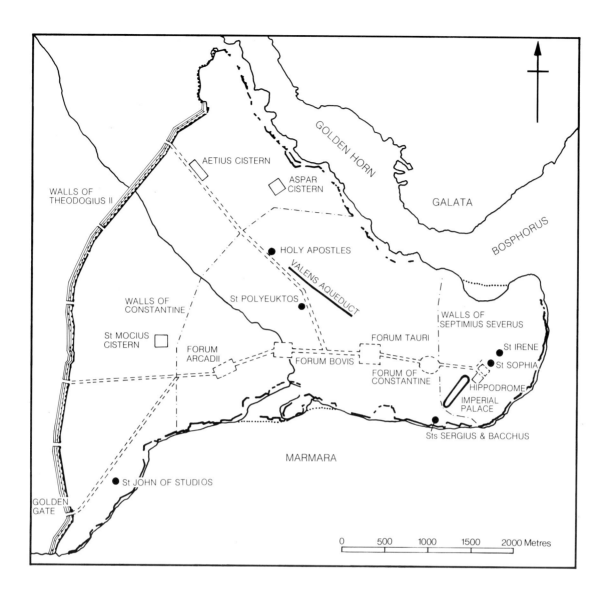

The Mesê was the main thoroughfare of the city; its approximate route is known, as well as the position on it of the piazza called Philadelphion. Now, the Forum of Theodosius (Tauri) is known to have been situated at Beyazit, and the Church of the Holy Apostles on the site of the great mosque of Fatih; Saraçhane where the blocks were found, lies about half-way between them (fig.30). That the site of Anicia Juliana's church had been discovered seemed tolerably certain, and it can be accurately dated to the years 524-527 from a combination of internal evidence in the poem and other historical testimonies. Here then was the opportunity to excavate and to study the remains of a 'lost' church of evident grandeur securely dated to the period immediately preceding the accession of Justinian and some ten years before St. Sophia.

*30. A plan of Constantinople showing the location of St. Polyeuktos on the processional route from the Forum of Theodosius to the Church of the Holy Apostles.*

Who was this Byzantine princess who 'surpassed the wisdom of Solomon' and 'raised a temple to receive God'? We know her chiefly from her portrait in the magnificently illuminated medical treatise of Dioscorides, which was produced for her and which is now in Vienna.[10] There, the strong, majestic pose of Anicia Juliana, enthroned between personifications of Magnanimity (Megalopsychia) and Prudence (Sophrosyne), commands immediate attention and authority (fig.32). And it is quite possible that the fine marble bust of a woman of this period acquired not so long ago by the Metropolitan Museum in New York, and said to have come from Istanbul, may also be a portrait of her (fig.33).[11]

Anicia Juliana's family was, quite simply, one of the most illustrious in the Roman Empire. On her father's side, she could trace her descent from men who had fought against Hannibal some seven centuries before, from whom statesmen of the highest calibre had sprung through the generations (see Family Tree, p.149).[12] In 472 her father, Flavius Anicius Olybrius, became one of the last Emperors of the West. On her mother's side, both her grandparents were directly descended from the Emperor Theodosius I: her mother Placidia was daughter of Valentinian III (son of Galla Placidia and grandson of Theodosius I) and of Licinia Eudocia (daughter of Theodosius II, granddaughter of Arcadius, and great-granddaughter of Theodosius I). Anicia Juliana herself was born about 462 and probably in 479 married one Areobindus, who was of German extraction. Their son was named Flavius Anicius Olybrius, after his maternal grandfather the Emperor, and he held the consulship as a child in 491, fifteen years before his own father, who only became consul in 506. Flavius Anicius later married Eirene, daughter of the Emperor, Anastasius I, and Anicia Juliana obviously hoped her son would ascend the throne. But when Anastasius died in 518, there was no clear successor, and the man eventually chosen was not Flavius Anicius Olybrius but Justin, an elderly uneducated soldier in the palace-guard who had started life as an Illyrian peasant. Even Areobindus had already failed his wife Anicia Juliana when he fled on being offered the throne in a popular riot in 512. Now, in 518, the accession of Justin I was clearly the last straw: the patience of one who was an aristocrat to her fingertips and whose blood was by four generations royal, snapped. No more is heard of Areobindus, who by now presumably had died. She, however, needed to make a concrete declaration of her own family's royal past and future; and this dynastic statement, as we shall see, was made in the form of the Church of

31. A peacock-arch from the main
entablature, with part of Line 30 of the
poem.

32 (overleaf left). Portrait of the Princess
Anicia Juliana enthroned between
personifications of Magnanimity
(Megalopsychia) and Prudence
(Sophrosyne). Detail from the
frontispiece of the great medical treatise
of Dioscorides, which was copied for her
in c. 512 and which is now in Vienna
(Nationalbibliothek, Cod. Vind. Med. gr.1).

33 (overleaf right). Marble bust of a
woman, found in Istanbul and now in
the Metropolitan Museum, New York.
Dated on stylistic grounds to the first
quarter of the sixth century, it may be a
portrait of Anicia Juliana.

St. Polyeuktos. The gauntlet flung down to Justin was picked up by his successor Justinian.

All evidence testifies to the grandeur of the church which Anicia Juliana added to her palace. In the poem (line 48) she is said to have surpassed Solomon, and it is noteworthy that, on the dedication of St. Sophia in 537, Justinian is said to have exclaimed 'Solomon, I have vanquished thee'.[13] For ten years St. Polyeuktos was the largest and most sumptuous church in the city, and it is tempting to suggest that Justinian's remark about Solomon with its implication of the Temple may have been, not simply a commonplace, but a sly reference to the eclipse of an erstwhile rival.

A story, told in the sixth century by Gregory of Tours, relates that on his accession Justinian asked Anicia Juliana to make a contribution to public funds.[14] She pretended to agree, asked for time to gather her treasure together, and meanwhile instructed her craftsmen secretly to hammer all her gold into plaques and to fasten them to the roof of St. Polyeuktos. When the appointed time came, Justinian went directly to her palace expecting to return with a substantial contribution. She took his arm (for she was old) and led him into the church, where, after they had knelt in prayer, she asked him to look up and see her treasure and told him to take what he wished. While he was covered in confusion, she took from her finger a ring which was adorned with a very large emerald and gave it to him, saying, 'Accept, most sacred Emperor, this tiny gift from my hand, for it is deemed to be worth more than this gold'. He took it and thanked her and returned to his palace.

If the story is not true it is at least *ben trovato*. The confrontation between the aged, wealthy and civilized aristocrat and the new Emperor, ending in the latter's discomfiture, looks like a set piece and certainly serves to illuminate what must in truth have been a real contrast. Perhaps, the story may even be taken literally. Anicia Juliana in 527 was an ageing woman, whose husband and son had failed her and who may have realized that she had not long to live (indeed she died the following year). Her principal *bête noir*, the illiterate Justin, was dead, and it is at least possible that she had decided now to accept the succession of Justinian as a *fait accompli* and even to confirm it. What is the meaning of the ring and of her curious statement about it? Was this ring her father's, when he was Emperor? Augustus, when he thought that he was dying, had handed his ring to his chosen successor, and later Hadrian had made a similar gesture. Perhaps the gift of the ring in her church was not the snub it first appears but rather the formal transfer of royal authority to Justinian as her acknowledged successor.

34. *Part of the main entablature of St. Polyeuktos; a niche with Line 31 of the poem, at the time of discovery in April 1960. The decoration, with peacock and twisting vinestem, is extraordinarily opulent and well executed, and the inscription enabled the block to be identified as part of the lost church of St. Polyeuktos.*

Political considerations apart, it was in any case immediately apparent that investigation of the church, firmly attributable to the three years before Justinian's accession and evidently large and sumptuously appointed, was a matter of importance and indeed, in view of impending development on the site, of considerable urgency.

*35. View of the site from the north-west corner, looking towards the atrium.*

# II · Excavation, Structure and Chronology

T HE SITE, in the district called Saraçhane, lay in open ground, in public gardens in the south-west quadrant of a major cross-roads, which was due to be transformed into an underpass. In 1964, as work on the underpass had begun, the Turkish Department of Antiquities issued the permit for excavation of the site jointly by the Istanbul Archaeological Museum and Dumbarton Oaks, and digging began on 4th August.

There were to be six campaigns: the first and last of one month's duration, the others of three. After the first season, supervisory staff regularly included Turkish students and museum and university assistants, and the labour force consisted almost entirely of villagers from Tokat in central Turkey, who regularly sought work in Istanbul before their harvest.

We worked from 7.30 a.m. to 4.30 p.m. six days a week, and the months spent on site were, in many respects, magical. Every season and almost every day yielded important material. Nezih Bey came each morning for an hour or two before his museum work began, returned most afternoons, and increasingly devoted his evenings and Sundays to helping us. His archaeological knowledge of Istanbul was unrivalled, and his questions, advice, help and encouragement were a constant inspiration. There were, too, extraordinary events: the carrying of the Olympic Flame across the site one afternoon in August 1964 on its way to Tokyo; the inadvertent uncovering on the blade of a bulldozer one morning in 1967 of cables carrying one half of Istanbul's electricity supply; and the flight each August of storks from Thrace to Anatolia in their tens of thousands! These were, however, exceptions, and the excavation, exposed as it was in the city-centre, proceeded with remarkable lack of distraction.

When we arrived, preparations for the underpass were well under way. The major north-south road on the east side of the gardens (the Atatürk Bulvari) had been closed and excavated to a depth of some five metres, and a temporary road to carry diverted traffic had been laid diagonally across the gardens (fig.36). No record had been kept of the precise find-spot of the marble blocks in 1960, and local conjecture as to where this had been varied by as much as 250 metres. The first task was to examine ancient masonry which had been exposed by bulldozers in the west face of the underpass cutting, the second to lay out a grid over the whole area against which our probes and finds could be plotted, and the third to open a series of exploratory trenches in the gardens. The grid was in five-metre squares designated alphabetically from East to West and numerically from North to South, and our trenches were generally 4 by 4 or 4 by 9 metres, with one-metre baulks between.

The underpass-cutting had clipped the eastern ends of two large rectangular structures, the southern consisting of a number of chambers with brick walls, tiled floors, and concrete foundations, the northern simply of stone-faced concrete (fig.36). The foundations of both structures, which stood three to four metres high, penetrated some five metres below present-day ground-level. In the narrow space between them were remains of an earlier tiled drain with intact cover-slabs. The drain had been cut by both

*36. General view, taken in August 1964 from the south-east, of the underpass cutting, our first trenches, and the temporary road. The solid structure projecting into the underpass proved later to be the foundations of the apse.*

37. An intact cross-vault in the
substructures of the north-eastern
corner of the church. Note the
levelling-course of large blocks from
which the vault springs and the
pointing with a mortar which contains a
high proportion of crushed brick.

structures, and the lower levels of its fill - silt from the period when it was still in use - contained sherds of distinctive red-slip pottery datable to the early part of the sixth century. The two structures thus appeared to be of the right period, as did a third on the same alignment which was encountered in trenches a short distance to the north, and which consisted of four vaulted chambers, two with the original vaults still intact (fig.37). That the third structure was contemporary with the first was suggested by the similarity of brick-stamps. Roman and early Byzantine bricks were frequently stamped with distinctive names or monograms, thus enabling them to be closely dated. The overwhelming majority (70%) of the stamps recovered from both structures recorded the third year of an indiction-cycle (fig.38). These cycles were fifteen-year fiscal

*38. Brick-stamp of cruciform type,
recording the third year of an indiction
cycle.*

45

periods, which had been introduced in 312, and it became common practice to date simply by reference to the particular year of the current cycle. The third year of one such cycle began on 1st September 524, precisely the year previously suggested for the start of Anicia Juliana's church. Associated finds, including fragments of mosaic, inlay, marble carving, and a colossal and elaborately-carved pier-capital (fig.23), could be attributed to the same date and also suggested to us that these could have been part of a church.

By the end of the first short season of excavation it appeared that the church had been found and that it lay under the gardens to the West, although exactly how the three structures related to it, and to each other, was not yet clear.[15]

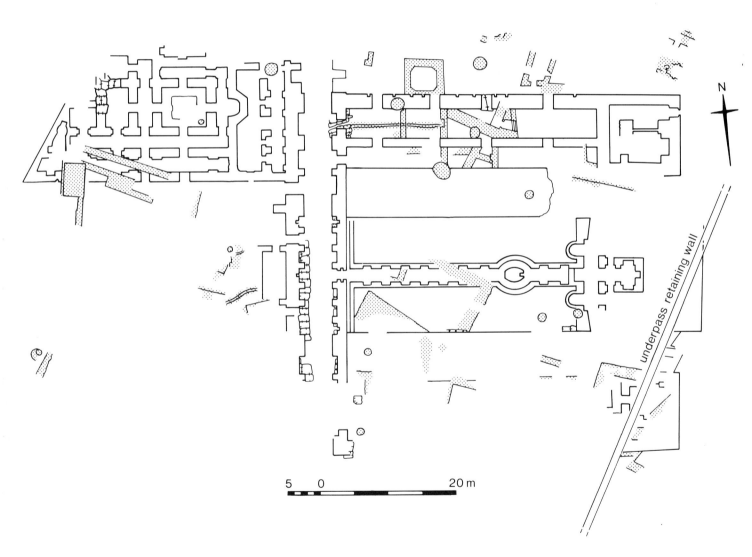

5   0                                    20 m

39. A simplified plan of the church as excavated.

40. A view, in 1964, of the gardens ➤ crossed by the temporary road and cut by the first trenches, looking north-west towards the Fatih Mosque (the Church of the Holy Apostles).

46

*41. General view of site of excavation
taken in 1965 during the second
campaign.*

*42. General view looking west, taken in
1969 during the sixth and last campaign.*

The answer came very early in the second season. It seemed possible that the three structures might together somehow constitute the eastern end of the church, and the church's north-east and south-east corners would thus be known. On the hypothesis that the church would have been rectangular and might perhaps have been square, a trench was opened west of the temporary road, to try to locate the north-west corner (if the church was square), or at least a part of the north wall (if it was not). A corner duly emerged, and the corresponding south-west corner was quickly found in a similar trench to the south. It was indeed the church, and the church was square (figs.41, 42). The rest of the second campaign was devoted to the selective exploration of nave, north aisle, crypt and narthex.

Although the remains of the church lay close to the surface, there were three main difficulties in tackling them. First, the eastern part of the church lay beneath an asphalt and concrete roadway, for the removal of which we had to borrow a pneumatic drill, and much of the rest of the site had been covered in 1960 by up to a metre of hardcore, which was very difficult to dig. Second, masonry survived to a height of about five metres above ancient ground-level, which meant that our trenches had to be very deep, particularly so for any examination of the foundations. Third, after the collapse of the church, the site had evidently been used to begin with as a quarry for brick and marble and then, from the late fifteenth century until very recently, it was occupied by Turkish houses and a small mosque. Although remains of the houses themselves, which had been of timber on shallow concrete foundations, were slight, their storage- and rubbish-pits everywhere penetrated Byzantine levels, like the holes in a sponge; the stratigraphy was extremely complicated, and progress often very slow.

The underpass was completed and opened to traffic in 1966, towards the end of the third season, and the temporary road that had now served its purpose was then closed. The two parts of the excavation could thus at last be united within one perimeter-fence (figs.42, 45). With more space now for manoeuvre, a bulldozer and trucks were hired early in the fourth season for the mechanical removal of the temporary road and the remaining hardcore. As the excavation continued, particularly in the western sector, the general lay-out and character of the church were becoming increasingly clear.

43. *A general view over the excavations from the south-east, taken early in the second season (1965). The main lines of the church were becoming clear, and work was concentrated on the area of the sanctuary (foreground) before construction began on a slip-road.*

44. *General view over the excavations from the south-east, taken at the end of the second season (1965). The apse-foundation (incorporated in the underpass-retaining wall) is visible, as are the north-east corner of the church (far right), the two passages beneath the north aisle, the trench in which the north-west corner was found (on the other side of the road), the great nave-foundation, and (in the left foreground) the crypt.*

General view across the excavations from the south-west, taken at the end of the third season (1966). Note that the cobbles of the temporary road across the church have been lifted and that a new bye-road has been constructed over the eastern part of the site. In the background the Aqueduct of Valens (378), the Süleymaniye Mosque (1550-57), and (with one minaret) the Tıramalı Medresse (1550).

General view at the end of the fourth season (1967). The great nave foundation, the two barrel-vaulted passages beneath the north aisle, and the southern end of the narthex are particularly clear.

In its simplest terms, the church was just under 52 metres square, excluding a narthex at the west end and a projecting apse-platform at the east end. To the west lay the atrium, part of whose marble pavement survives, with a range of buildings on its northern side. All that remains is substructure, for the floor of the church had been raised about five metres above the ground, and this has been skimmed off in successive levellings of the site. The principal access from the atrium had been by a great staircase, of which the foundations and lowest step survive. The church was divided into central nave and side-aisles by two colossal foundation-walls, which would have supported *inter alia* the nave-colonnades (fig.48). Two parallel barrel-vaulted passages supported the floor of the north aisle (figs.47, 48), and there was a similar system for the south aisle. The nave-floor was supported on a solid packing of clay topped by a thick layer of marble chips, except along the axis, where a narrow underfloor passage gave direct access from the narthex-substructure to a square crypt beneath the sanctuary (fig.44). The crypt consisted of a small room with a marble floor surrounded on three sides by a passage with a tile floor, and there appear to have been staircases leading down to it from the sanctuary above (fig.53). At the exact centre of the church, this passage divided to pass a curious elliptical foundation of concrete, which presumably served to support the ambo (pulpit) (fig.54). The north-east and south-east corners of the building each had a complex of barrel– and cross-vaulted rooms (figs.51, 52), and the narthex substructure was similarly roofed by a combination of barrel- and cross-vaults (fig.49).

The rectangular apse-platform was of solid concrete faced with stone, and the two massive nave-foundations, each about eight metres thick and deep, were also of stone-faced concrete with one

*47. A stratigraphic section across the north aisle, looking east. Note the north wall and the outside drain, the two barrel-vaulted passages, the conjectural level of the aisle floor, which was above modern ground-level, and the thickness of the massive foundation between aisle and nave.*

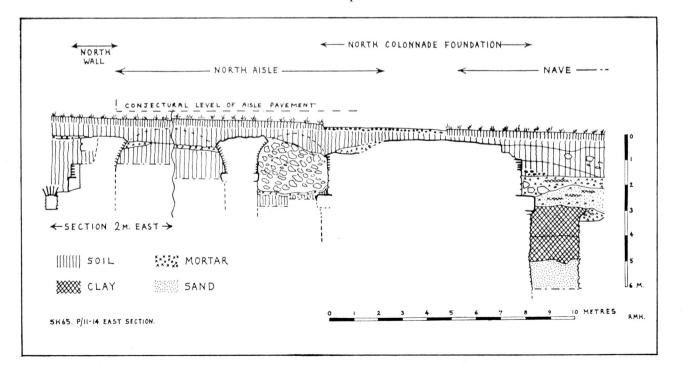

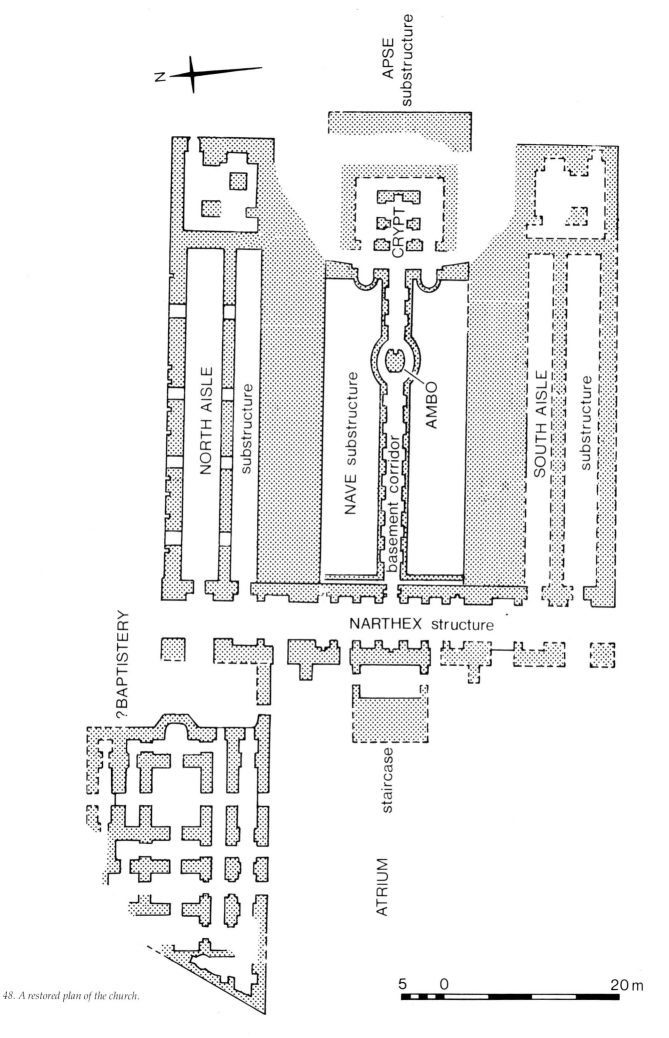

N

APSE
substructure

CRYPT

NORTH AISLE

substructure

NAVE substructure

basement corridor

AMBO

SOUTH AISLE

substructure

NARTHEX structure

?BAPTISTERY

ATRIUM

staircase

*48. A restored plan of the church.*

5   0                    20 m

53

49. *The inner face of the
outer wall of the narthe*
*substructure, during
excavation of its northe*
*sector, from the
south-east. Note the tw*
*stone-courses separated
by ten of brick, and the
narrow marble
string-course at the
springing of the vault.
The terracotta drain-p*
*is one of four which in
tenth century were cut
into the fill which had
accumulated over the*

levelling course of large stone blocks and another of brickwork. The wall-foundations of rough concrete were cut some three metres into natural sand and capped by a course of large dovetail-clamped blocks. On these blocks the walls were constructed, of concrete faced with neat, squared, well-dressed stones and laced with bands of brickwork, or (in the outer wall of the narthex) of brick with levelling courses of stone (fig.49). Bricks are generally between 35 and 40cm. square and about 4.5cm. thick, and mortar beds, often pointed with a particularly hard mortar which has a high proportion of brick-dust, are generally of similar thickness. Many bricks are stamped, but the exact function of these stamps, which are circular, square, oblong or cruciform, is not known. Some include indiction-numbers, which, as mentioned above, refer to a date.

Substructure-walls were generally capped by a thin chamfered course of marble, from which sprang barrel- and cross-vaults (fig.49). The bricks in these vaults are generally somewhat smaller (and thus lighter) than those in the walls.

The substructures were choked with fallen debris, including substantial marble pieces, and any reconstruction of the super-structure will depend on a study of these, within the constraints of the excavated plan and the poem in the Palatine Anthology (figs.48, 169). Only one part of the superstructure survived — a brick-pier of about forty courses fallen flat on to the atrium pave-ment, presumably from an upper storey of the church's western façade (fig.50).

*50. Part of a fallen upper-storey pier in the atrium. Note the cornice block with alternating conch-and-cross decoration.*

51. *The southern of the two parallel barrel-vaulted passages which supported the north aisle, in course of excavation, from the east. There are areas at the western end and in the centre which have not yet been dug. In the foreground are short pieces of wall on an oblique alignment, which antedate the church.*

*52. The northern passage beneath the north aisle, looking west. This has been excavated to sixth-century ground-level and the walls, whose brick vaults carried the aisle-floor about five metres above ground level, penetrate some three metres into subsoil. Note the massive foundation-course of what is in effect the west wall of the church. (See also colour illustration, Fig. 64).*

53
54

*53 (left). The crypt, from the south-east. This lay beneath the sanctuary. A central room was paved and revetted in marble, while the surrounding passage had a tiled floor and plastered walls. (See also colour illustration, Fig. 66).*

*54 (below left). The foundation of the ambo (pulpit) and the wall of the passage beneath the nave, from the south.*

*55 (right). The passage beneath the nave during excavation, looking west, with block carrying part of line 9 of the inscription, palm tree pier and fallen fragments of inscription, line 16.*

*56 (below). The passage beneath the nave, looking east with the palm tree pier, the block carrying part of line 9 and the ambo foundation.*

55

56

We found that the building was particularly well provided with drains (e.g. fig.57). Vertical pipes in slots in the outer face of the church's north wall (fig.78) carried rainwater from the roof into a deep drain with cover-slabs westwards along the outside of the wall and into the smaller of two parallel brick-vaulted drains running south beneath the floor of the narthex substructure (figs.60-62). These latter drains were also fed by vertical rainwater-pipes in the inner and outer walls of the narthex (figs.58, 59) and by a pair of converging channels from the inner faces of the two great nave-foundations, which also seem to have had vertical feeders. The direction of flow of the drains showed that the church had been built on the southern slope of the ridge, and the incidence of the down-pipes gave some clues as to the form of roofing.

*57. The substructure of the north aisle, looking west, showing an original drain.*

*58 (opposite page, above). The west wall of the church during excavation and the western end of the axial passage which ran beneath the nave. Note the blocking of the passage, and the immured drainpipe, which discharged into one of the vaulted drains beneath the narthex. To the right of the ranging pole, are the timber-laced concrete foundations of a substantial early Turkish building, probably the Karagöz Mosque (c. 1493).*

*59 (opposite page, below). Detail of inner east wall of narthex-substructure, from the west, showing the massive foundation-course, and the slot for a drainpipe. Five courses of brick are followed by four of neatly squared stone, followed again by brick (not seen here).*

58

59

60. *The narthex-substructure in course of excavation, from the south. The left-hand ranging-pole stands at floor-level (visible as a light line in the section). The right-hand pole stands in one of the two large drains; the vault of the other can be seen to the left.*

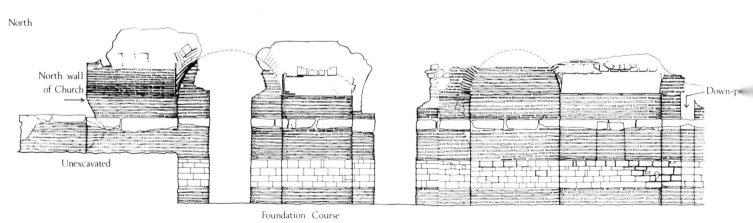

North

North wall of Church →

Unexcavated

Foundation Course

Down-p

62. *Elevation-drawing of the inner wall of the narthex- substructure, looking east.*

61. A view, from the north, of the larger (western) of the two vaulted drains running south beneath the floor of the narthex. There were inspection-covers at regular intervals. The pairs of stone corbels, each pair placed midway between the two nearest opposite pairs, cannot be explained, but presumably had some service function.

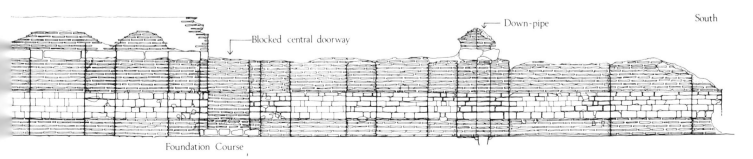

South

Down-pipe

Blocked central doorway

Foundation Course

In the atrium several paving-slabs of marble remained *in situ* around the vaulted foundation of the great staircase, and of the staircase itself part of the lowest step survived (fig.68). To north and south of the staircase, doorways led down by four steps into the substructure of the narthex (fig.67), giving direct access by the axial passage to the crypt. The passage was, however, at a fairly early stage carefully blocked at both ends with neat brickwork (fig.63); it may perhaps still have been accessible by a trap in the ambo. On the north side of the atrium was a complex of substructures which overlooked it and which incorporated the supporting walls of a square apsidal building with some sort of central basis (figs.69, 70). This may have been a baptistery, for the substructure-vaults of the central square chamber were lower than those of the surrounding passage, implying a main floor with a sunken centre; the basis is inferred from the hollow shaft in the middle of the room, which appears to be connected to the drainage-system. In any case, there was presumably direct access from the main floor of this building to the main floor of the church. The western wall of this complex was at an oblique angle to the others, suggesting that there may perhaps have been an earlier street here on a different alignment (fig.71). Unfortunately, the western end of the atrium was completely destroyed in Ottoman times, and similarly nothing survived on the south side. If there was a matching southern complex, the width of the atrium would have been 26 metres, just half that of the church. This is in essence the structure of Anicia Juliana's church.

*63. Inner wall of the narthex, from the west, showing the careful blocking of the passage beneath the nave.*

*64. The north passage under the north* ➤
*aisle looking west, excavated to*
*sixth-century ground level.*

65. *The inner face of the western wall of the narthex, from the north-east. Note the broad foundation-course flush with the narthex-floor.*

66. *View of crypt, looking north-west.*

*67. Northern stairs down from atrium into narthex-substructure*

*68. Substructure for staircase from atrium to main church-entrance, from the north. Several slabs of the original (white Proconnesian) marble pavement survive.*

69. *General view of the substructures north of the atrium, from the south.*
*The marble blocks (right foreground) have been laid out on the level of the atrium pavement.*

< 70. *Substructures of apsidal square building (Baptistery?) to north of atrium, from the south. In the eleventh century some doorways and passages were blocked, the walls were covered with plaster, and the complex converted into a cistern.*

Λ 71. *The west end of the substructures on the north side of the atrium, from the south-west. The acute angle is curious and probably reflects an earlier building-line or street. Note the immured downpipe for rainwater.*

72. *Gravestone of a Gladiator, third century A.D. This is from the Roman cemetery which is known to have lain in this area, outside the walls of the pre-Constantinian city. Height 0.50 metres.*

Naturally, we were also looking for traces of settlement earlier than the church, including any vestiges of the fifth-century building which, according to the poem, it replaced. The church's massive foundations, however, cut deep into natural sand, restricted the areas where earlier remains could be sought. But several third-century Roman tombstones, including one of a gladiator (fig.72), were found in early levels within the north-aisle vaults and are evidence for a cemetery here in pre-Constantinian times, when the district lay far outside the city. Very short lengths of wall were found beneath the nave and the north aisle, and at a deep level just outside the north-east corner of the church, all on a markedly different alignment from that of the church itself (fig.51). But they could neither be related to each other nor could they be closely dated. Much more substantial were the foundations of two parallel east-west walls lying beneath the north side of the atrium, which were cut by a brick-vaulted north-south drain; this also underlay the atrium pavement and is thought to have been contemporary with the church. Both walls, which were exactly aligned with the church, were associated with fifth-century deposits, and they were evidently part of a large building, which determined the alignment of the church but had to be demolished or curtailed to accommodate it. This building may have been part of the palace, to which the church was annexed and which probably lay on this northern side. There is no evidence that any of these earlier walls belonged to the fifth-century predecessor of St. Polyeuktos mentioned in the poem.

The site, which sloped as it does now from north to south, was levelled before construction of the church and prepared with a thick layer of black clay (fig.47). The foundations of Anicia Juliana's church were cut through this and into the underlying sand. Pottery associated with the construction includes groups from the fill of a drain cut by the apse, the make-up of the nave-floor, the underpinning of the atrium-pavement, the mortar of the pier found fallen into the atrium, and the mortar from the north wall of the atrium. Although only one coin was found in these layers (a worn specimen probably of Justin I), coins of Justin I (518-527) were generally frequent in other early layers, implying some particular activity then (fig. 73). As for the brick-stamps (fig. 74), an analysis of recorded indictions shows one cluster of third- and fourth-year examples and another of twelfth- and thirteenth-year examples, the latter including all the light bricks, which are assigned to the superstructure. The years 524/525 and 525/526 were the third and fourth years of one indiction-cycle and correspond nicely with the period when the church is thought to have been under construction; that there are no examples of the fifth year would simply mean that construction was completed in about two years and that work was now concentrated on interior decoration and furnishing. The other cluster is presumably attributable to the years 518/519 and 519/520 and represents old stock; a less likely hypothesis is that they represent a major repair to the church (following a collapse of the dome?) after Anicia Juliana's death.

*73. Bronze coin of Justin I .*

*74. Three brick-stamps, including two circular monograms and one cruciform stamp, mentioning a third year (probably 524-525).*

There is, in fact, very little evidence for any structural modification or repair. The first clear alteration was the careful bricking-up at both ends of the axial passage. That narthex and crypt remained accessible is indicated by the careful exterior finish to this blocking (fig.63). A number of small deposits, particularly at floor-level in the western section of the northern north-aisle substructure are evidence for some activity in the substructures in the second part of the sixth century or early part of the seventh century. About the middle of the seventh century the levels just mentioned were sealed by a huge mixed deposit of dumped material, and there were considerable further deposits in the eighth to tenth centuries. Whether the church remained in use as such is simply not known, although it was on the Emperor's Easter itinerary in the early tenth century according to the *Book of Ceremonies*,[16] which was a list of the official duties of Emperors drawn up by Constantine VII. The interior of the church was accessible to the editor of the Palatine Anthology at about the end of that century, as we know from a marginal note in the manuscript.[17]

Considerable quantities of rubbish accumulated during the late tenth and eleventh centuries over the atrium-pavement, in the

*75 (opposite page). Cistern built in substructures north of the atrium, from the south-west. The arch is in the outer wall of the narthex, and in the eleventh century it was blocked and the piers and pilasters inserted to carry vaulting over this part of the cistern.*

*76. The northern part of the atrium during excavation, from the north-west. The further ranging pole stands against the substructure of the great staircase and upon remains of the sixth-century marble pavement, which was quarried in the twelfth century. A part of the bottom step of the staircase is still in position. In the foreground, beyond the measuring rod, is a group of subsequent twelfth-century graves. On the right and overlying the graves are the remains of a brick pier fallen from the superstructure of the church.*

vaulted space beneath the staircase, and over earlier fills in the narthex. Its compact nature and the high proportion of crushed pottery, animal-bone and carbonized remains, makes it probable that there was a squatter-occupation in and around the atrium. In the twelfth century the complex of substructures north of the atrium was converted into a cistern (fig.75). Stone foundations underlying the northern part of the atrium were robbed, presumably to provide stone for the cistern construction. The atrium now became a cemetery, which appears to have remained in use for a considerable time, with some graves cut by later burials (figs. 76, 77). By the early thirteenth century the church lay in ruins.

*77. Close-up of graves in Fig. 76, looking east.*

78. A trench cut against the outer face of the north wall of the church, from the north. Note the alternation of brick and stone in the wall and the slot for a drainpipe, which discharged into a large drain covered with stone slabs. In the foreground is a large stone-lined pit of Turkish date.

79. The remains of a base for a staircase, in the atrium.

80

81

# III · Decoration

ANICIA JULIANA spared no expense in the construction and embellishment of her church, the like of which had not been seen. As her construction-workers finished the shell of the church, their places on the scaffolding would have been taken by the decorators — sculptors, mosaicists and workers in revetment and inlay. This change-over, which marked the beginning of the final phase of work on the church, probably took place in 526.

Internal walls were panelled with marble revetment and rich inlay, the curving surfaces of vaults decorated with mosaic, and marble piers, capitals and entablatures enriched in fantastic variety with sculptural carving. Not until the forest of scaffolding had been removed would the floor have been laid and furnishings provided for nave and chancel.

Small fragments of wall-revetment were recovered in enormous quantity. Materials included the following: red porphyry from Egypt, green porphyry from the Peloponnese, a particularly hard yellow marble (*giallo antico*) from Chemtou in Tunisia, a green breccia (*verde antico*) from Thessaly, a black marble flecked with white from the Pyrenees (*celticum*), a purplish marble streaked with grey and white from Iasos in Caria, various kinds of creamy white and dappled white marble from Dokimion in Phrygia, a pinkish pudding-stone from Bilecik in Bithynia and, of course, abundant white marble from Proconnesus (figs.80, 81).[18]

Proconnesus is an island in the Sea of Marmara, whose northern half consists of white marble usually streaked with greyish blue. It was quarried from early classical times, and later, under the Roman Empire, Proconnesus became a major producer, not only supplying the needs of the region, including Byzantium and its successor Constantinople, but also exporting widely to the cities of the Black Sea, the Levant, Tripolitania and Italy. Coarser than Docimian and cheaper than the exotic coloured marbles, Proconnesian was used for the narrow beadings which, sometimes plain, sometimes decorated with bead-and-reel or dentil ornament, framed the revetment panels. It was also the principal material for architectural elements and marble furnishings for the church.

◄ *80. Fragments of marble revetment. From top left, clockwise: red porphyry from Egypt, green porphyry from Laconia (southern Greece), yellow (giallo antico) from Numidia (Algeria), green breccia (verde antico) from Thessaly (northern Greece).*

◄ *81. Fragments of marble revetments. From top left, clockwise: Proconnesian; celticum (from the Pyrenees), Iasos (south-western Asia Minor), Bilecik puddingstone (Bithynia), dappled Docimian (Phrygia), and white Docimian (also Phrygian).*

There were, too, more elaborate panels of fine inlay mounted with an adhesive (probably bitumen) on slate. Serrated leaves of mother-of-pearl, strips of yellow glass with gold leaf, and an abundance of pale green and dark blue opaque glass cut into rectilinear and curvilinear shapes, were combined in prefabricated panels with small, finely cut pieces of shaped marble, particularly red and green porphyry and *giallo antico*. These panels are comparable with panels in St. Sophia in Istanbul, S. Vitale in Ravenna, and the Basilica of Euphrasius in Porec (Parenzo).

In the area of the chancel were found six fragments of inlaid columns, two with some of the inlay still precariously adhering (figs. 82, 83, 94). Squares of amethyst are framed by triangles and trapeziums of opaque green glass to form hexagons; there are canted squares of amethyst outside the hexagons, and diagonal runnels contain strips of gold glass. The columns, which vary in diameter from 35 to 41 centimetres, were probably from the ciborium (baldacchino) above the altar.

The church's excavated debris yielded an abundance of mosaic embedded in small fragments of plaster which had fallen from the apse and other vaults. Tesserae are mainly of glass, with occasional use of marble, limestone, and terracotta (fig.92, 93). Of several thousand fragments recovered, only thirty-five were attributable to figures. Of the rest, a few might be from garments, but the overwhelming majority were either plain or had simple designs (circles, triangles, arcade, etc.). Abstract designs clearly predominated, and dark blues and greens were the most frequent colours. Of the figured fragments, all but one came from the area of the

*82. The upper part of an inlaid column as found fallen in the area of the sanctuary. The design is of green glass, gold glass and squares of amethyst, and the column is thought to have been one of four which supported a canopy above the altar.*

*83. Part of an inlaid column, which has lost its glass inserts.*

apse, which also produced a large quantity of plain gold ground. The apse evidently included figures set against a gold background, and one fragment shows the lower part of a face, with neckline, bearded jaw, chin and mouth, rather less than life-size (fig.93). The gold background has sixth-century parallels in the monastery of St. Catherine on Mount Sinai, the Panagia Kanakaria in Cyprus, S. Vitale in Ravenna and, if indeed its mosaic is of this date, the church of St. George in Thessalonica.

84. Marble-waste re-used as make-up of the nave floor, evidence that the architectural sculpture was carved on the site. (Length of largest piece 0.09 metres.)

Scraps of pavement-mosaic from the nave were also found. The material was marble (white from Proconnesus, yellow from Numidia, green from Thessaly, and black from the Pyrenees) set in a rectilinear geometric design. The tesserae were set in plaster, which itself overlaid a deep stratum of masons' chips. The nave was at least partially paved in geometric mosaic (in its south-eastern sector); masons' chips covered the whole of the nave; this suggests that the mosaic may have extended over the same area.

There is good stratigraphic evidence that the vault-mosaic belongs to the church's construction-period, and this sixth-century date gives it a singular importance in view of the almost total destruction of figured mosaics in Constantinople under the rule of Iconoclasm in the eighth century. This is the first figured vault-mosaic of the sixth century discovered in Constantinople.

Revetment, inlay and mosaic might be expected in a Constantinopolitan church of this period. What was entirely unexpected, however, was the character of the architectural sculpture, astonishing in its novelty, variety, abundance and sheer technical quality. Equally remarkable is the way in which it was so widely dispersed. The derelict church was looted during the Fourth Crusade by the Frankish army, which in 1204 turned aside from its appointed task and laid siege to Constantinople; and important pieces of carving then found their way to the west — to Venice, Barcelona, Aquileia, and even Vienna (see figs.111, 118, 128, 129).

With very few exceptions the material is Proconnesian marble, which arrived for the most part in roughly shaped blocks.[19] New quarries would have been opened for the purpose, and material shipped in an unfinished state; the carving would have been done on site and, in the case of the more elaborate pieces, even after the blocks had been hoisted into their final position. That the work was done on site is proved both by the large quantity of marble waste (fig. 84) which served as packing for the floor of the nave and by several unfinished pieces (fig. 112); that the detailing was done when the block had already been hoisted into position is proved by the differential use of the chisel, for the final stages were sometimes omitted in corners which could have been dark or inaccessible (fig.85).

Technically, the sculpture is of the highest order. It is remarkable as much for its underdrilled lattice- and strap-work as for its exuberant vegetation virtually detached from the background, especially the carefully carved and delicately chiselled vine-leaves.

Outstanding are the superbly modelled peacocks, which are practically in the round. The workmanship is nowhere hesitant or painstaking; rather, it conveys the impression of masterly, swift and confident execution, as indicated particularly by marks of the chisel, by small irregularities, and by the springing line of lattice-bars, which are not strictly rectilinear but deftly carved by eye.

Originally, the sculpture was painted, and traces of bright blue pigment have remained in the background of several blocks. Other bright colours, including gold, may be imagined. Add the polychrome revetment, elaborate inlays, mosaic, and metal ornaments, and the chromatic effect must have been rich indeed.

In any description of the sculpture, pride of place must go to the magnificent entablature, flanking the nave and carrying the first forty-one hexameter lines of the dedicatory poem which is preserved for us in the Palatine Anthology. The fragments discovered consist of niches, arches and corner-blocks, each inscribed and thus attributable to specific parts of the poem. Above the inscription, which is in raised letters 11 cm high, is a twisting grape-vine, carved in extraordinarily naturalistic detail, each leaf with raised veins, the edges of the leaves carefully underdrilled at an angle of about 45°, and some leaves fading into the background in an attempt to suggest a third dimension. Every niche was filled by

86. A peacock-niche from the main entablature, with part of Line 31 of the poem (see also Fig. 34). (Height 1.44 metres, actual width 2.26 metres, restored width 2.75 metres.)

87. A peacock-niche from the main entablature, with part of Line 32 of the poem. (Height 1.435 metres, width 1.15 metres.)

88. A peacock-niche from the main entablature, with part of line 30 of the poem. (Height 1.44 metres. actual width 1.494 metres, restored width 2.80 metres.) See also colour illustration Fig. 31.

89. A peacock-arch from the main entablature, with part of Line 25 of the poem. (Height 0.765 metres.)

a large peacock shown frontally, with tail outspread and body carved in the round. The soffit of each arch contained two such peacocks confronting each other, their tails almost touching at the crown of the arch and their heads close together, beak to beak or cheek to cheek. We found two pieces of claws, clasping a small rounded boss which projected at the springing of the arch, as well as several bodies, necks and fragmentary heads (figs.90, 91); towards the crown of the arch is the scar of the peacock's shattered crest where it touched the feathers.

The lines of the dedicatory poem provide an excellent tally. For instance, one of the pieces originally uncovered by bulldozer in 1960, a niche, carried line 31 of the poem (fig.86). Subsequently, two arches were found in the excavations, with lines 30 and 32 (figs.87, 88). The three blocks — arch, niche and arch — were thus adjacent, and, moreover, the face of each block presented a slight concave curve in plan. Together they constituted the major part of an open curvilinear exedra (semi-circular bay), which had a diameter of between 6.5 and 7 metres. One other niche (line 16) was found, and one arch (line 25) (figs.89, 96, 97). Traces of bright blue pigment survived in the background of the inscription of the arch with line 32. This colour survived also on several other pieces of sculpture, although all trace of other colours had disappeared.

*90. The right eye of a peacock. Note the traces of the crest. The pupil was probably of translucent green glass. (Length 0.133 metres.)*

*91. The body of a peacock, broken off from an arch or niche of the main entablature. (Length 0.52 metres.)*

92. Five fragments of vault mosaic, each with a white rosette against a black or red background.

93 (below left). Figured mosaic from the area of the apse. Three joining fragments make up the lower part of a face, with neckline, bearded jaw, chin, mouth, and part of left nostril. The mouth is partly indicated by paint. The scale is about three-quarter life-size. The importance of this figure lies in its rarity, in view of the wholesale destruction of figured mosaics in the eighth century.

94 (below). Part of an inlaid column at the moment of lifting, with much of its inlay (squares of amethyst, triangles and trapeziums of green glass, and in the diagonal runnels, strips of gold glass) still precariously adhering.

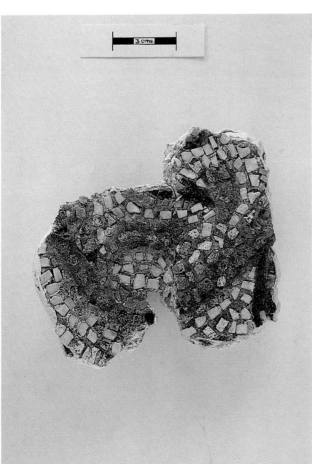

95 (left). A detail of the arch shown in Fig. 88. The background of the inscription was painted blue, but other colours have not survived. The naturalism with which the twisting grapevine was carved is quite extraordinary at this date.

96. A peacock-niche from the main entablature, with part of Line 16 of the poem.

97. Part of a peacock-niche joining with the broken piece in Fig. 96, which carries Line 16 of the poem. Note the carefully moulded soffit (underside) of the block, which shows that it spanned columns or piers.

98. *Corner-block of main entablature, with part of Line 27 of the poem. Note the erect and pendant vineleaves on this face which were framed in a diagonal lattice; the adjacent (left-hand) face has an overall twisting vine. (Height 1.335, width of left face 0.955 metres, width of right face 0.825 metres.)*

99 *(on opposite page). Corner-block of main entablature with part of Line 9 of the poem. Note that one side of the block is decorated with an informally twisting vinestem, while the adjacent face has a more formal scheme of pendant and erect single leaves in a diagonal lattice. Note too that the inscription emerges from a broad low arch. (Height 1.46 metres.)*

Two corner-blocks were found, each decorated on two adjacent faces. On one (line 27) the left-hand side is decorated above the inscription with the familiar twisting grapevine, while the right has a more formal design of undercut diagonal lattice, in the interstices of which are alternately pendant and erect vine-leaves (fig.98). On the other (line 9) it is the right-hand face which has the twisting grapevine, but enough of the left-hand face is preserved with its diagonal lattice to show that the inscription was carried over a broad low arch (or niche) in this face (fig.99). It is evident that in each case the corner-block marks the springing of a curvilinear exedra (twisting vine-stem) from a straight, more formal face (lattice). There appear to have been three exedrae on each side of the nave, and these seven inscribed pieces hold the key to any reconstruction of the church's lay-out and elevation, as we shall see later.

100. The right-hand end of a cornice or hood, decorated with circular monograms, between the modillions, and two kinds of palmette, both of which are of Sassanian design. (Length 2.23 metres.)

The marble blocks discovered by chance in 1960 included two types of cornice, both with monograms and both probably better described as 'hoods' for doorways. A block of the first type was found in our second excavation-season, at the western end of the nave, beside a large threshold which was thought to be from the main doorway between narthex and nave (figs.100, 103). Above two minor mouldings is a series of circular monograms, alternating with modillions, each of which has a split-palmette with pendant pomegranates. A row of stylized plants runs above these, and here two semicircular leaves curve inwards, enclosing a central lyre-shaped element beneath two superimposed rows of pellets.

The pieces of the second type combine to form a gigantic block, 2.45 metres long, the left end of which is missing (figs.104, 105). One sliver was found in the excavation, also in the western part of the nave. At the bottom is a fillet with a simple rinceau of trilobate leaves; a roundel with kidney-shaped plants (derived from the egg-and-dart), each consisting of three pairs of incurving sharply serrated leaves; on the horizontal part, monograms in circular frames alternate with modillions, each of which carries a split palmette supporting a stylized tree; the corona displays a bizarre, deeply undercut scheme (figs. 104, 105). From a stunted base emerge two feathery leaves and above them, again to left and right, two cornucopiae; from these sprout sinuous stems, each with three strands: one turns in to link up with its neighbour, to support a pendant seven-lobed leaf between the two cornucopiae; the third reaches the upper edge of the corona, where it emits a feathery

101 (below left). Detail of the sprig-and-leaf cornice (Fig. 107). Blue paint was noted in the lobes of the leaves.

102 (below right). Chamfered cornice with a simple repeating motif which seems to be based upon a stylized egg-and-dart. (Height 0.12 metres.)

inturning leaf. Along the lower edge of the corona, between each pair of cornucopiae, runs a strand of ivy, with a leaf at each end and a third leaf erect at mid-point, immediately beneath the pendant five-lobe leaf.

A third type has a quarter-round moulding, sometimes decorated with alternating crosses and deep scallop-shells, sometimes plain (fig.106). In one block there are traces of bright blue pigment behind the lobes of the intact shell and in the surrounding penannular groove. That it was used in the upper storey is shown by its occurrence in the upper-storey pier found collapsed across the atrium (fig.50).

Another cornice or impost has a repeating motif of an upright nine-point sprig set against (or growing within) a nine-lobed 'leaf', alternating with a sprig of nine small leaves (figs.101, 107). The lobes of the large 'leaf' are deeply concave, rather like the flutes of a scallop-shell, and retain traces of bright blue pigment. Among other cornices we discovered one with an alternating lotus-and-palmette scheme, and another with what seems to be a stylized egg-and-dart (fig.102).

*103. Detail of the cornice in Fig. 100.*

104. *Part of a monogram-cornice or hood. (Length 1.375 metres.)*

105. *Right-hand end of the monogram-cornice or hood in Fig. 104.*

106. *Quarter-round cornice from an upper storey, decorated with an alternating scheme of conch and cross. Traces of blue paint were observed in the conch. (Length 0.57 metres.)*

107. *Cornice, decorated with an alternating leaf-and-sprig design, the seven-point sprigs alternating with nine-lobed leaves against which are set nine-point sprigs. (Height 0.26 metres, length 1.335 metres, width 1.05 metres.)*

*108. Basket-capital decorated with a distinctive split-palmette which is framed by undercut interlace. (Height 0.695 metres.)*
*See also colour illustration, Fig. 124.*

At least four types of basket-capitals adorned the columns. One example of each has survived in tolerable condition, as well as many hundreds of small fragments which can be assigned to one or other of the types.

The first is a basket-capital with undercut interlace framing a trapezoidal panel on each side (fig.108). Each panel is adorned with a split-palmette consisting of an erect three-lobed form between two sinuous leaves, rising from a T-shaped base. From the base also spring, to left and to right, two nervously undulating lines which terminate in a sub-rectangular element. The motif, apparently used here for the first time, became fairly popular in the sixth century, and it is found, for example, in Ravenna, Poreč, and Varna.[20] The interlace, underdrilled and detached from its background, was meticulously executed, although much of it has been broken away. Three similar capitals from the same series are to be found in the façade of San Marco in Venice, removed with much else from the ruins of St. Polyeuktos, in 1204 or soon afterwards, by members of the Fourth Crusade (fig.125). Another basket-capital is decorated with a diagonal lattice, framing in each square a cross with diagonal rays and delicately flaring arms

(fig.110). A large rectangular stud marks each junction of the lattice separated by three small round studs on each lattice strip. The carving is deeply undercut, being attached to the core of the capital only at the centres of the crosses and the junctions of the lattice. The upper border, a formal interlace set with small flowers, is not undercut. The third basket-capital is badly damaged, but it was decorated on at least two sides with a tall slender stylized vase from which emerge two twisting vine-stems; the first swirling curve on each side of the vase holds not a leaf but an eight-point star (fig.109). A scar at the corner of the capital shows that the two surviving sides were separated by an openwork border.

*111. Basket-capital in the Barcelona Archaeological Museum which has been shown to have come from the church of St. Polyeuktos. Note the broken boss at each corner of the abacus and the broken cornucopiae below; originally each boss was supported by openwork, but this has been broken. The myrtle leaves represent medieval re-working of a scar. (Height 0.92 metres.)*

Finally, we turn to a magnificent basket-capital in the Archaeological Museum at Barcelona, which has been shown to have come from St. Polyeuktos (fig.111).[21] Like other pieces, it left Constantinople presumably at the time of the Fourth Crusade. Its base moulding is decorated with large ovoid forms (each having a Latin cross in relief) alternating with erect trilobate leaves, which are linked by a stem passing beneath the leaves. The crown moulding is decorated with a row of trilobate plants, each lobe with a pellet at its tip, and each plant having in addition two pendant pepper-like fruits. The principal design on each face of the capital consists of three superimposed cornucopiae set centrally, from which issue, splayed to left and to right, two elaborate sprigs of acanthus. The

112. *Two joining fragments from the excavations of an unfinished capital similar to that in Barcelona. The design has been masked out with a drill; the background has still to be struck away and the surfaces finished with a chisel. This is evidence that the architectural carving was done on the site. (Overall length 0.285 metres.)*

113. *A fragment from the excavations of a capital similar to that in Barcelona (Fig. 111).*

acanthus and much of the other carving is deeply underdrilled. The corners of the capital have been badly damaged. Projecting bosses at the corners have in each case been smashed, but the twin stumps of cornucopiae, above the base moulding beneath each corner are evidence of elaborate openwork which must have embellished each corner to support the boss. The vertical bands which formed the background to the openwork, in three out of four cases, must have been re-worked as myrtle sprigs in the thirteenth century. The connection with St. Polyeuktos was proved by the discovery in our excavations of several pieces of an identical capital (or capitals) (figs.112, 113).

114

114 (above). Pier-capital identical to those of the so-called 'pilastri acritani' in Venice, which have been shown to have come from the church of St. Polyeuktos. Note in particular the broken cornucopiae and the damaged corners, where originally there was undercut foliage supporting projecting bosses. (Height 0.90 metres.) See also colour illustration, Fig. 147.

115 (left). Detail of pier-capital in Fig. 114, showing the rebate which occurs in one corner.

116 (above right). Pilaster-capital which had been bonded into a wall. (Height 0.76 metres.)

117 (below right). Pier-capital of St. Polyeuktos type recently found re-used in a Turkish context at Edirnekapi, near the Theodosian Land Walls. (Height 0.82 metres.)

115

116

117

*118. The western pier of the 'pilastri acritani' in the Piazzetta at Venice. See also colour illustrations, Figs. 122, 148*

Two types of pier-capital were evidently used, and again we found one very fine specimen and many fragments of each. The first has on each side an elaborate scheme of an extremely stylized plant, with a central vertical stem from which emerge symmetrically to left and right sinuously undulating stems; from the latter springs a further stem with two tendrils, one of which encloses a vine-leaf, the other a six-point star (fig.114). To lower left and lower right, on the central stem, and at the topmost tip of the two flanking stems, are helical elements or whorls, five in all. The two principal flanking stems are apparently supported from the main stem by two descending rods, which dominate the scheme incongruously, like a gigantic circumflex accent. The base moulding is decorated with eggs alternating with trilobate leaves, and the upper moulding has a series of simple split-palmettes. At each of three corners of the capital there was a projecting boss supported by openwork springing from a pair of cornucopiae beneath the corner; at the fourth corner there is a small rectangular rebate, from base to top, and there were two pairs of cornucopiae from which sprang two systems of openwork, separated by a groove and supporting two bosses. This capital was found in the first season and is identical with those of the two so-called *pilastri acritani*, which stand in the Piazzetta in Venice (figs.118, 122).[22] Although they were long supposed to have come from Acre in Palestine in 1258 (hence the nickname), they were in fact taken from St. Polyeuktos, presumably in or soon after 1204. A fourth capital of this series was recently discovered; it had been re-used in a Turkish building near Edirnekapi in Istanbul (fig.117).[23] And in our excavations we came across a similar design on an engaged pilaster-capital (fig.116).

The other pier-capital, which is somewhat larger, has a central date-palm on each side flanked by a twisting plant with spade-like leaves and eight-point flowers; the upper border is adorned with a row of three-lobed elements, the lower border with a scheme of protuberant eggs (each with a cross) alternating with trilobate leaves (fig.150). Again, projecting bosses were supported by openwork at each corner, and again at one corner there is a rebate.

The two types of pier-capital, were matched by two types of pier. The smaller is best described by reference to the two *pilastri acritani*, which, like their capitals, can be shown to have come from St. Polyeuktos (figs.122, 123). Each pier has an upper border of diagonal strapwork; the upper half of the shaft has a richly-decorated panel on each face, and the lower half is plain on three sides; on the fourth is a simple rectangular panel with a cross-and-orb. On two sides the decoration of the upper half is a formal scheme of

two similar designs, set one above the other. In each design there is a circular monogram, which cannot unfortunately be read with confidence; it is set centrally between a large pendant vine-leaf above and an erect vine-leaf below; to left and to right are vertical scrolls of smaller vine-leaves alternating with bunches of grapes. On the other two sides the design consists of a cantharus (vase) from the pedestal of which rise two thick vine-stems forming a large erect vine-leaf and coming together to support a pomegranate at the top; from these stems spring, alternately, bunches of grapes and vine-leaves. There is a rebate along one edge of the shaft, corresponding with the rebate in the pier-capitals. One fragment from the excavations is the upper corner of such a pier (fig.120). A pilaster found built into Turkish foundations near the site of the church, carries a similar design, as does a slab in the Istanbul Archaeological Museum, which was found in Koca Mustafa Pasa Camii (formerly the Church of St. Andrew in Krisei). Both of these must have come originally from St. Polyeuktos (fig.119).[24]

*119. Upper part of a pier or pilaster, found in the Koca Mustafa Pasa Camii (formerly the church of St. Andrew in Krisei) and now in the Istanbul Archaeological Museum. This piece is clearly of the same series as the so-called 'pilastri acritani' in Venice and presumably also came from the church of St. Polyeuktos. (Height 0.645 metres.)*

*120. Upper part of a pier, with border of inclined fret and a central pomegranate flanked incongruously by a bunch of grapes and a vineleaf. This matches exactly the sides of the so-called 'pilastri acritani' in Venice. (Height 0.615 metres.) See also colour illustration, Fig. 146.*

*121 (above right). Upper part of a pier, with upper inclined-fret border and main panel with twisting vinestem. A frame of open flowers has been introduced, for this pier was distinctly wider than the so-called 'pilastri acritani'. It is thought to have supported the palm-tree pier-capital (Fig. 150). (Height 0.54 metres.)*

The second type of pier is represented by an upper corner piece, which has a moulding of diagonal strapwork above a border of rosettes that encloses the main panel with a thick twisting stem (fig.121). Whereas the first type had an upper width of 88cm, exactly corresponding with the lower edge of the smaller pier capital, the second type now had a width, when restored, of 1.10m, exactly corresponding with that of the palm-tree capital. Thus we may form a very good idea of the decoration. In a piece recently discovered in the Basilica at Aquileia, there is a large cantharus within a rosette-border, with a foliate base beneath an open ring composed of simple small out-turned leaves; above is a large pendant vine-leaf, and to the left and right the remains of subsidiary feathery leaves (fig.128).[25] It appears to be of Proconnesian marble and, in view of similarities of motif and technique, is likely to have come from St. Polyeuktos. It would have reached Aquileia from Venice.

122. Two piers and their capitals in the Piazzetta in Venice. Although they are traditionally said to have come from Acre in Palestine in 1258 and have thus been known as the 'pilastri acritani', they are now shown to have belonged to the church of St. Polyeuktos in Constantinople, from whose ruins they were taken in the Fourth Crusade.

123. Detail of the western pier of the 'pilastri acritani'. Note, above, diagonal strapwork, and below, circular monograms, each set between a large, naturalistic pendant and erect vineleaf. These leaves spring from a double stem, and borders to left and right are filled by a simple scroll with alternating vineleaves and bunches of grapes.

124. *Basket-capital with split-palmette discovered in the excavation.*

125. *Split-palmette capitals in the south-west corner of the basilica of San Marco in Venice, which are thought to have belonged to the church of St. Polyeuktos.*

126. *Fragmentary screen of Docimian marble, re-used in the church of the Pantocrator (Zeyrek Camii), with a repeated motif of a stylized cantharus from which emerges a strap-like stem with superimposed hearts and banana-like fronds.*

127. *A selection of screen-fragments from the excavation, of the same series as those in the church of the Pantocrator (Fig. 126). See also colour illustration, Fig. 145.*

128. *Fragmentary slab in Aquileia, with stylized cantharus, pendant vineleaf, feathery leaves, and a border of open flowers. This appears to be from a pilaster or a pier of the kind which supported the palm-tree capitals in the church of St. Polyeuktos.*

129. *A screen of Docimian marble in the Kunsthistorisches Museum in Vienna. This item came to Vienna from Venice in the nineteenth century and was thought to be a piece of fourteenth-century Gothic architecture. It is in fact an original screen from St. Polyeuktos heavily reworked (there are many tell-tale traces of this) in the fourteenth century. (Length 1.75 metres.)*

The Zeyrek Camii in Istanbul (a twelfth-century building which was formerly the church of the Pantocrator) has in its Turkish fittings a number of fragmentary screens of soft yellowish-white marble from Docimium in Phrygia (fig.126).[26] The principal design is a repeating motif of a stylized cantharus, from which emerges a strap-like stem with superimposed hearts and banana-like fronds. Between one cantharus and the next is an upright border set with alternately round and square studs, the latter with lentoid pellets attached diagonally at each corner. The upper border has a scheme of grape-clusters alternating with eight-petal flowers, each suspended from a simple interlinking stem. These pieces provide the key to a large number of small fragments from the excavations of what were clearly identical screens (fig.127), and it is certain that these, too, were taken from St. Polyeuktos.[27] A full screen had three cantharus-panels, as is known from an unbroken but heavily re-worked example which is in the Kunsthistorisches Museum in Vienna (fig.129). This screen, which reached Vienna from Venice in the nineteenth century, would have been reworked in Gothic style in the fourteenth century. It corresponds exactly in material (Docimian marble), measurement, design and technical detail, with the pieces in Istanbul, and its original provenance is not in doubt.[28] Fragments of many other screens of Proconnesian marble came to light. The majority were of a standard sixth-century type with, for example, a six-arm cross within a wreath flanked on each side by a cross-and-orb, but there were pieces, too, of several more elaborate screens, including one with a border of everted triangular leaves surrounding two interlaced squares containing a monogram (fig.130), another with alternating lozenge- and key-motifs (fig.131), and four with remains of openwork were also discovered.

*130 (below left). Fragment of a screen with two interlaced squares containing a monogram, in a rectangular frame with a border of everted triangular leaves. (Height 0.37 metres, length 0.114 metres.)*

*131 (below right). Fragment of screen with a lozenge- and key-pattern border. (Height 0.32 metres, length 0.28 metres.)*

132. Part of a frieze with a hook-motif between bead-and-reel borders. (Height 0.26 metres.) The distribution of the thirty-one fragments of this frieze suggests a location in the sanctuary (see caption to Fig. 133).

In addition a large number of fragments of two narrow friezes were found, most of them in the area of the chancel and apse. One of these is decorated in shallow, flat relief with a cross-in-arcade motif, each bay strictly separated from its neighbour, while the other has a repeating yoke-motif; both have a bead-and-reel border above and below (figs.132, 133).

133. Part of a frieze with a cross-in-arcade motif between bead-and-reel borders. (Height 0.305 metres.) Forty-two fragments of this frieze were found, thirty-seven of them in the area of the sanctuary, to which the frieze should be ascribed.

*134. Wall-panel, from the area of the apse and slightly curved in plan. The plants, three in each register, are highly stylized and of Sassanian derivation. (Height 1.62 metres.)*

More spectacular were very many fragments of at least three wall-panels. These were slightly concave in plan, in three zones, the upper and lower of which are decorated in relief, the central being left plain (fig.134). The two decorated zones are closely similar: each has a row of three stylized plants. From a simple three-lobed leaf resting on three pellets rises a central stem crowned by a small egg-shaped flower above three more pellets. This is flanked by two graceful, feathery leaves, which spring not from the base of the main stem, but from the lateral lobes of the base leaf. These feathery leaves curve out, each to touch the top of the one next to it, and the two tips together supporting a small supine crescent against the upper edge of the zone. The central lobe of the base leaf is backed by a slightly larger version of itself, and the veins of the leaves are shown simply, in fine relief.

Another remarkable discovery was that of a series of small figured panels, all in a late-Byzantine level in the narthex and all systematically defaced. In each case the surface at the back is polished (suggesting that the panels decorated some sort of screen), and each one is pierced in the lower centre by a dowel-hole which may have been for fixing, or for a pin from which something might be suspended. The defacement of these panels which from their context must be pre-Turkish is most easily attributable to the ravages of Iconoclasm in the eighth-century, when religious images were systematically destroyed by order of the Emperor. This would then be a *terminus ante quem* for the reliefs, and there seems no reason not to assign them to the sixth century. After their defacement they were presumably salvaged and put into store, so that their find-spot may bear little relation to their original location.

The series comprises a bust of Christ, represented with a halo encircling a cross, hair to shoulder, a medium-length pointed beard, the left hand draped, and holding a book with cross and studs, the right hand held across His chest; a bust of the Virgin, also with halo, holding in front of her the upright figure of the Infant Christ; and busts, some of them fragmentary, of eight Apostles, four with books, one holding a staff with cross over his left shoulder, none of them with haloes (figs.135-142). The lack of haloes may be thought to favour the early date proposed.

*135. Fragment of bust of Apostle. (Width 0.415 metres.)*

136. *Marble icon with bust of Christ. This and the other icons in the series had been systematically defaced, probably by Iconoclasts in the eighth century. (Height 0.38 metres.)*

137. *Marble icon with bust of the Virgin and Child. (Height 0.36 metres.)*

138. *Marble icon of an Apostle, called Apostle A. (Height 0.375 metres.)*

139. *Marble icon of an Apostle, called Apostle B. (Height 0.38 metres.)*

*140. Marble icon of an Apostle, called Apostle C. (Height 0.38 metres.)*

*141. Marble icon of an Apostle, called Apostle D. (Height 0.36 metres.)*

*142. Marble icon of an Apostle, called Apostle F, his right hand raised in blessing and his left holding a cross-staff. (Preserved height 0.37 metres.)*

143. *Capital of small engaged column, carved in one piece with the shaft. The motif on the front of the capital is an erect oblong frame containing superimposed chevrons; from the outer edge of the frame spring tongue-shaped leaves. On the sides the design is repeated. (Height 0.45 metres.)*

Architectural elements recovered in the course of excavation included a number of carved fragments which may conveniently be grouped together here. One is the top of a boar's-head water-spout, with snout and front of crest quite clear and eyes well modelled (fig.156). Another is a hooked beak, possibly of an eagle, broken off where it would have joined the head and drilled through at the inner corner of the upper and lower beak, presumably for suspension (fig.158, left). A third is a piece with stiff straight wing-feathers, not from a peacock but perhaps again from an eagle (fig.158, right). As well as pieces of five small birds in high relief, evidently from the inhabited scroll of a capital or other carving (fig.144), there were large numbers of pine-cones, cornucopiae (in two sizes), bunches of grapes, acanthus and other leaves, and eggs, all in very high relief. Mention may be made, too, of the capital of an engaged colonnette, which was cut in one piece with the shaft. The motif on the front is an erect oblong frame containing superimposed chevrons; from the outer edge of the frame spring at the middle of each side a tongue-shaped leaf, and at each corner a narrower leaf with a pellet at its tip. Above and below the leaf in the middle of the long side springs a leaf whose tips curl in to enclose a pellet (fig.143).

144. *Fragment of a small bird in high relief, probably from some 'inhabited' foliage. (Length 0.095 metres.)*

145. Screen fragments discovered in the excavation, similar to those used in the Church of the Pantocrator (Zeyrek Camii).

146. Upper part of a pier discovered in the excavation, matching exactly the design of the sides of the 'pilastri acritani' in Venice.

147 (overleaf, top left). Pier-capital discovered in the excavation.

148 (overleaf, below left). Pier-capital of the western pier in the Piazzetta at Venice. The carving is of the sixth century, except for that at the angles, beneath the bosses, which is thirteenth-century reworking of broken area.

149 (overleaf, top right). Basket capital with undercut lattice discovered in the excavation.

150 (overleaf, below right). Pier-capital with central date-palm discovered in the excavation. Note the damaged corners, where undercut foliage had supported projecting bosses. (Height 0.93 metres.)

147

148

149

150

151. *The shattered remains of two window-frames and other marble pieces, as found fallen into the cistern north of the atrium, from the north-east.*

152 and 153. *A window-frame reconstituted from seventy joining fragments (many of them in Fig. 151). (Height 2.53 metres, width 0.88 metres, thickness 0.11 metres.) On analogy with St. Sophia, the panes would have been 3 × 9. In any case, St. Polyeuktos, like St. Sophia was highly fenestrated.*

We catalogued more than ten thousand pieces of marble, and made brief notes on many others. The overwhelming majority were undecorated except for mouldings. They included cornices, columns, bases, thresholds, door-frames, window-frames, plinths, posts, screens, skirting, beading and gutters. With very few exceptions (a plinth and a screen of *verde antico*, a screen of *celticum*, posts of alabaster, and a plinth of red porphyry), the marble was Proconnesian. Two window-frames, which had fallen into the substructures of the building north of the atrium, could be reconstructed, one from fifty-six fragments, the other from seventy (figs.151-153). This was, however, exceptional. The site had been so badly robbed that very little mending was possible. Of the seventy-six lines of the poem, only parts of seven survive, less than five per cent of the complete text. Most of the window-frames were found to be rectangular, a small minority semicircular, and from the number it is clear that the church was, like St. Sophia, highly fenestrated. The paucity of window-glass suggests that the church was systematically stripped of its panes for cullet.

The marble material was particularly distinctive and important. From ancient sources we know of various marble-cutting techniques. The principal tools were the chisel (fig.157) and the drill (fig. 155). The latter, which was used initially to prick out the design (fig.112), was of course the bow-drill, an iron point in a wooden shaft which was rotated by the oscillation of a taut bowstring twisted several times around it. Its extraordinary accuracy can be seen in the undercut strapwork which frames the design of the split-palmette capital and which is entirely detached from its background (fig.149). The drill would have been held diagonally at an angle of about 45° and oxidized tips of several broken points of iron (diameter 2-3 millimetres) were found embedded in the marble. There is similar use of the drill in the undercut lattice both of the lattice-capital and of the main entablature (fig.108). The

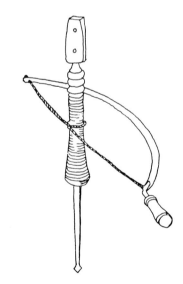

155. Reconstructed drawing of a bow-drill. The iron drill and wooden handle are from Egypt; the bow is a reconstruction. (After D. Strong and D. Brown.)

*156. Boar's Head water-spout. One of several water-spouts found, one with a lion's head, the others plain.*

sculptors knew instinctively the tolerance of their brittle material, and the accuracy of the probing drill is like that of the modern dentist. The drill was also used for undercutting the edges of vine-leaves on the main entablature (fig.98) and generally for other foliage, including openwork supporting the corner-bosses of several capitals, and for eggs, pine-cones, cornucopiae and many other features. One of the reasons for assigning the exotic screens of Docimian marble to the church's original fittings is that they show a similar use of the drill to undercut the banana-like fronds and to cut the background (fig.145).

The chisel was used to dress all visible surfaces: flat backgrounds, the simple friezes (figs.132, 133), the diagonal strapwork

*157. The mason's principal tools (flat chisel, mallet, and point) carved on the side of a Roman sarcophagus, which has itself been dressed with a claw-chisel, at Marcianopolis in Bulgaria.*

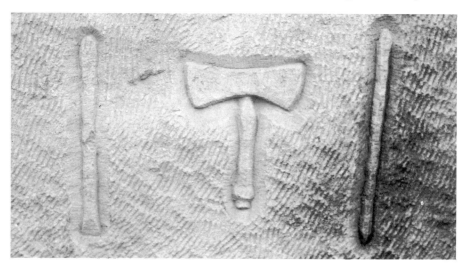

*158. Left: The beak of an eagle. Note that, at the break, it has been pierced for suspension. Right: A fragment with feathers, which are quite unlike those of the peacocks and may be attributed to the eagle. (Length of beak 0.015 metres, of feathers 0.145 metres.)*

which crowns the piers (fig.121), the inscription of the main entablature, and underdrilled strapwork and lattice. It was also used for such decorative features as the peacocks, eggs, cornucopiae, pinecones, and the twisting vine-stems and carefully modelled vine-leaves.

The sculptural motifs we encountered ranged from the most classical to the most exotic, sometimes in juxtaposition on the same block, sometimes too in combination in the same design. As already noted the irregularly twisting vine-stem within each exedra had underdrilled leaves delicately modelled with raised veins, some leaves merging into the background to suggest a third dimension (fig.95). This extraordinary naturalism is in the mainstream of Hellenistic and Roman tradition, reminiscent even of the Ara Pacis of Augustus at Rome. The corner-blocks of the exedra have each on one side an undercut diagonal lattice, in the interstices of which are set alternately pendant and erect vine-leaves, each naturalistically carved but each now set within a formal scheme (fig.99). Similarly, each marble pier exhibited on two opposed sides a formal scheme, wherein a large pendant vine-leaf was suspended above a circular monogram, while a similar vine-leaf rose beneath it; both were carved with great naturalism but both sprang from a split stem, which formed regular rinceaux up the sides of the panel, with smaller, carefully arranged vine-leaves and bunches of grapes set alternately (as in figs.119, 123). On the

159. Vine-leaf. Detail of corner block decoration found in excavation.

160. Detail of twisting grape-vine from a peacock-arch of the main entablature. There was some evidence of blue paint. (See also colour illustration, Fig. 95).

other two faces of each pier, two twisting vine-stems with naturalistic leaves and bunches of grapes grow up from an elaborate
cantharus, uniting at the top of the panel to produce, incongruously, a ripe pomegranate (as in figs. 120, 122).

Each exedra accommodated five large peacocks, their tails outspread, their bodies, necks and heads carved in the round, their
feet in high relief on short pedestals. One bird set frontally occupied the central niche, while two faced each other across the flanking arches, the tail-feathers rising to the crown of the arch to touch
the headcrest. Each peacock had a necklace in low relief; there is
evidence to suggest that the eyes may have been of green glass (a
small sphere of translucent green glass, like a child's glass marble,
was found to fit neatly into an eye-socket); the marble was probably richly painted, not only in blue, but also in red, green and
gold, and a chain may have been suspended from the beak. Earlier
examples of protuberant animals and birds (protomes) in sculpture occur in oriental contexts at, for example, Persepolis, Hatra
and Baalbek.[29] Perhaps the most remarkable occurrence, however,
of peacocks carved in the round, is at Memphis in Egypt, where a
pair in limestone adorned the Hellenistic approach to the so-called
Serapaeum, their tails outspread, rising from a bed of twisting
vine-stem, and their bodies each straddled by a figure of the young
Dionysos.[30]

*161. Peacock feathers from the main
entablature with inscription (broken).
The body of the peacock may have
resembled Fig. 91.*

162. *Sassanian decorated plaster from the villa at Ctesiphon. Berlin, Staatliche Museen.*

In sharp contrast with the identifiable naturalistic plants, birds and animals, an extensive range of stylized plants, palmettes and other exotic devices was used as embellishment. The source is clearly Sassanian Persia, the great power on Byzantium's eastern frontier which had a long tradition and rich repertory of such distinctive forms. Although the originals may have been in monumental sculpture or stucco, the motifs were transmitted at second hand, by silks, ivories and metalwork.[31] Apparently things Persian were fashionable in Constantinople in the first part of the sixth century, and it is perhaps significant that Areobindus, Anicia Juliana's husband, had commanded the Byzantine forces against Persia from 503 to 505, and having seen action in Mesopotamia and Persian Armenia, had returned to Constantinople with considerable booty.[32] We may suppose that his booty included textiles, which doubtless adorned the palace, and that they generated at home a taste for Persian designs.

Parallels for the more exotic motifs in the church of St. Polyeuktos are found not only in Persian but also in Umayyad (that is, early Arabic) art, particularly in the Dome of the Rock at Jerusalem, the Great Mosque at Damascus, and the so-called desert-palaces in Jordan and Syria. These parallels are useful and indicate that they and St. Polyeuktos owe much to common (Sassanian) sources.

Two kinds of palmette on one of the monogram-cornices (fig.100) were reminiscent of such Sassasian elements, as were the palmettes and feathery leaves displayed on the other cornice (fig.104), and the feathery splayed leaves, delicate and symmetrical, of the pier-capitals in Venice (fig.148). The fanciful nature of plants in this category may also be illustrated by the curved wall-panels (fig.134).

And again a stylized vase, a strap-like stem with superimposed hearts, and banana-like fronds (fig.145) were found on a series of screens; the stem of hearts also occurs in Sassanian and Umayyad art, and the fronds recur in Umayyad. Furthermore, there are Umayyad parallels for the repeating motif of a sprig set against a leaf, found on one of the St. Polyeuktos cornices (fig.163).[33]

The particularly strong Sassanian influence is felt when comparing a lattice capital at St. Polyeuktos (fig.110) with an actual Sassanian capital now in Teheran: only here flowers mark the interstices instead of crosses.[34] The split-palmette capital (fig.165), too, employs a Sassanian motif, although there was a telling misunderstanding by the sculptor when it came to depicting the two 'tendrils' with their carefully cut, irregular undulations — which, whatever they are, are surely not vegetable. It is probable that confusion arose here between the so-called Sassanian ribbon, which is a regular feature of Sassanian art and which, in the stucco decoration of a palace at Kish, is used to tie a split palmette, and the irregularly undulating stream of living water which, in many

*163. Leaf ornament from cornice. Detail of Fig. 107.*

*164. Stylized cantharus. Detail of Fig. 126.*

*165. Split palmette leaf from basket capital, Fig. 124.*

periods of Mesopotamian art, moves into and out of the Tree of Life.[35] The kinds of textile by which such motifs may have been transmitted from Persia to Constantinople can be exemplified by a silk in Aachen (fig.166).

On the excavation we sometimes felt that we were uncovering not a church but a museum, for the range, variety and number of motifs is truly enormous. As we have seen, four distinctive types of basket-capital, two kinds of pier-capitals, and at least six types of decorated cornice are represented. Add the main entablature, inlaid columns, wall-panels, posts and screens, and it seems unlikely that any one building in Antiquity ever approached St. Polyeuktos in profusion of ornament. The overall decoration of piers, pilasters and wall-panels appears to be without precedent.[36]

Another remarkable feature of the church is the rejection of classical mouldings and their traditional forms of decoration, particularly for the entablature. Little use was made of the ovolo moulding with its egg-and-dart, little of the roundel with its bead-and-reel, and none at all of the *cyma reversa* with its erect acanthus, or the acanthus-scroll frieze.

Finally, a word may be said about figured sculpture. The small rectangular panels with busts of Christ, the Virgin and Child, and various Saints are, as we have seen, almost certainly pre-Iconoclast and probably of the church's first period (figs.135-142). Traces of plaster along the edges of each panel show that they were set in some sort of frame, and a rectangular dowel-hole near the bottom edge of each was either for a clamp to secure the panel to its frame or, more likely, for a projecting pin from which, for example, a lamp might have been suspended. It is not known where in the church they were placed, but one possibility is that they adorned a templon or iconostasis. Admittedly, the style is simplified and less competent than that of the architectural carving. But it is highly likely that these panels, too, were of the sixth century and thus of Anicia Juliana's conception.

*166. Fragment of Persian silk-textile in the Treasury of Aachen Cathedral.*
*Persian textiles were highly prized in Byzantine Constantinople, and it is suggested that Persian motifs*
*were transmitted by textiles and other portable objects.*

167

# IV · Reconstruction

THE CHURCH'S SURVIVING SUBSTRUCTURES provide the outlines of its groundplan, and the debris preserves tantalizing remains of its superstructure. It is highly probable that there was a dome but, before considering this further, we should look at the plan in more detail and find evidence for the elevation.

In plan (figs. 48, 169) the church is square, with an apse projecting to the East and a narthex added to the West. Within the square, two broad and deep foundations which run from West to East, divide the building into, as it were, nave and aisles. The area of the north aisle is occupied by two parallel barrel-vaulted passages which would together have supported the aisle-floor, and the south aisle was similarly supported. In the north-east and south-east corners of the building, the substructures contained identical groups of chambers. The floor of the nave had been carried for the most part on solid packing, and down the centre ran an under-floor passage leading from the narthex-substructure to a rectangular crypt. The passage enclosed, exactly at the centre of the church, the foundation for the ambo. We thus have a square plan with a central feature and with internal division into nave and aisles; we also have the deliberate elevation of the church-floor and the width and depth of the two gigantic nave-foundations, which presumably supported the colonnades between nave and aisles and any piers.

Into this simple plan of known dimensions must be accommodated the great inscription. Although only fragments survive, the full text, preserved, as we have seen, in the Palatine Anthology, enables us to place the fragments in relation to each other. The poem had a total length of seventy-six lines, and we know from the note in the manuscript (see illustration on p. 6) that the first forty-one were inscribed around the nave. Parts of seven of these lines were recovered (fig. 168), and the entablature-blocks on which they were carved are of three types: arches, niches and corner-pieces.

◂ *167. Reconstruction drawing of the interior of St. Polyeuktos, looking east towards the apse.*

*Corner, with part of line 9 (detail of fig.99)*

*Niche, with part of line 16 (detail of fig.96)*

*Arch, with part of line 25 (detail of fig.89)*

*Corner, with part of line 27 (detail of fig.98)*

*Arch, with part of line 30 (detail of fig.31)*

*Niche, with part of line 31 (detail of fig.86)*

*Arch, with part of line 32 (detail fig.87)*

Lines 27 and 31 had been uncovered by bulldozers in 1960, and their exact find-spots were not recorded. The other five, however, were found lying as fallen in clockwise sequence, indicating that the inscription started in the south-eastern corner of the nave. Line 9 lay just west of the ambo, and line 16 a short distance west again, both in the axial passage; lines 25, 30 and 32 lay from west to east within the substructures of the north aisle.

The three blocks carrying lines 30, 31 and 32 had evidently been contiguous, forming an arch-niche-arch sequence. The face of each of these three blocks presents a shallow curve in plan, and it is clear that together they constituted the central part of an open curvilinear exedra (semicircular bay), which had a chord of about 6.5 metres. The face of the blocks is decorated, above the inscription, with luxuriantly twisting vine-stems, and these vine-stems recur on the two corner-blocks (lines 9 and 27), which may thus be assigned each to the corner of a similar exedra. The other decorated

169. Diagram of proposed lay-out of the Church, explaining the sequence and direction in which the poem in the Palatine Anthology was inscribed, and the location of the seven surviving lines of the poem (fig. 168). Also shown are four semi-circular bays (two on the left, two on the right), and four tower supports.

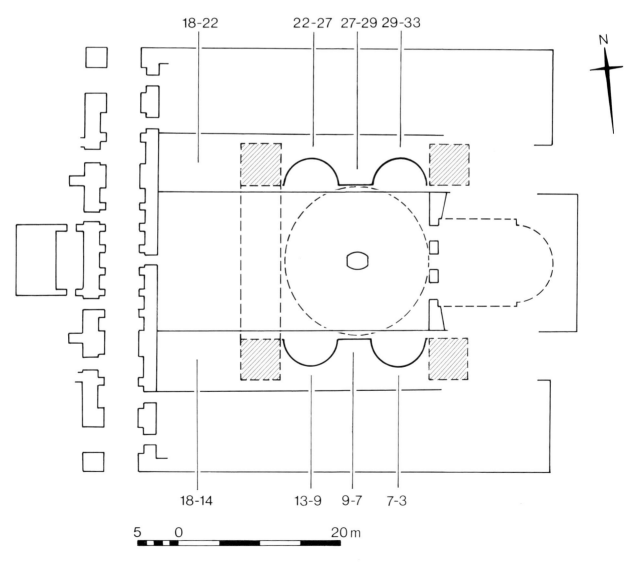

face of each corner-block, however, carries a different design, of a diagonal lattice framing, alternately, pendant and erect vine-leaves. Line 9 adorns the left-hand corner of one exedra, and line 27 the right-hand corner of another. On the corner which carries line 9, the face with the diagonal lattice is broken off at the springing of a wide arch, and the original length of the block is estimated to have been about 4.50 metres. It seems that this wide arch, whose face was straight in plan, not only preceded a curvilinear exedra but also succeeded one, which would have carried the first few lines of the poem. We thus have a pair of curvilinear exedrae separated by a straight element on the north side of the nave, and a corresponding pair on the south side (fig.169).

The eastern end of the nave is marked at substructure-level by a cross-wall, which may also have marked the line of a chancel-barrier above. This cross-wall lies 9.25 metres east of the ambo-foundation, which is at the exact centre of the church. If the two pairs of exedrae are set centrally on the two broad nave-foundations, these faces will each be about 9.25 metres from the church's central axis. If each pair is centred on the ambo, there is room for a central square bay of about 9.25 x 2 = 18.50 metres. The combined lengths of the two exedrae (13 metres) and their two outer ends (say 1 metre) and the straight element linking them (about 4.50 metres) also come to 18.50 metres and could thus define the northern and southern sides of such a bay. This square bay would be defined by four piers set on the massive foundations, and this hypothesis would help to explain the extraordinary thickness and depth of these foundations, which would thus carry not only the piers but the deep exedrae between them.

Lines 16 and 25 would then be accommodated in single exedrae on the south and north sides respectively of a western bay, and a central square bay over the eastern part of the nave would allow room for this narrower bay and two additional piers. If it is objected that in this scheme the inscription is not continuous, it may be observed that the inscription is part of a very elaborate entablature, and that the corresponding elaborate entablature (uninscribed) in St. Sophia is also interrupted, being confined to the nave colonnades and exedrae.

Although no recognizable fragments of a dome have survived, a number of factors suggest that the church was indeed domed. The sheer size of the foundations is evidence for an abnormally heavy superstructure and, although there is a longitudinal scheme of nave and aisles at floor-level, the square (rather than oblong) ground-plan suggests a centralized (rather than oblong) roof-system. The position of the ambo, in the eastern part of the nave but at the exact centre of the church, goes further to support this. Its central position will only have been apparent if it stood exactly beneath a central tower or dome, and that it stood in the middle of a square bay, which would have been required for a tower or dome, is, as we have seen, indicated by the surviving elements of the inscribed entablature. Open curvilinear exedrae, moreover, have often been a characteristic of centralized buildings, as, for example, in the so-called Piazza d'Oro of Hadrian's Villa at Tivoli in the second century, and in the martyrium at Seleuceia Pieria in the fifth century. The *Palatine Anthology* itself may indeed provide some evidence for a dome, for there it is stated in lines 55-57 of the poem about this church: 'On either side of the central nave, columns standing upon sturdy columns support the rays of a golden roof'. The upper columns were, of course, those of the gallery, but the Greek word for ray (*aktis*) is unfortunately ambiguous, for it is not clear whether the reference is to the radiating ribs of a golden dome or simply to rays of light. The combination of longitudinal ground-plan with centralized superstructure had already appeared in the provinces, most notably perhaps in a group of churches in Isauria in the latter part of the fifth century, and it was to be perfected by Justinian in his great domed church of St. Sophia in 532-537. St. Polyeuktos was by any account an ambitious, novel and extravagant building, and a dome in this context will come as no surprise.

The real problems occur not in plan but in elevation. Exedrae, remains of which were excavated, are attested also by the poem (line 58), and so are galleries (line 56). The exedrae were thus presumably of two storeys. On the hypothesis of a square central bay, the four masonry piers would have carried four great arches, one across each side of the square. The northern and southern arches would each either have been filled by a wall, as in St. Sophia, or developed into a barrel-vault, as in St. Eirene. On either system, the eastern and western arches would have opened into cross- or barrel-vaults over the chancel and the western part of the nave. If the northern and southern arches opened into barrel-vaults, there would have been, both inside and out, a cruciform scheme around the central bay.

Some evidence for the roofing is provided by the drainage. There were down-pipes in both inner and outer walls of the narthex in its central sector, implying that the narthex-roof in this sector had a valley and externally visible vaulting, rather than a single pitch. Similarly, the water-channels which run westwards within the inner faces of the great nave-foundations were presumably fed by down-pipes in the principal piers, suggesting a system of valleys between the nave-roofing and that of the aisles.

The palm-tree pier-capital (fig.170) and the fragment of its supporting pier (fig.121) were found lying close together in the axial passage with a corner-block of the inscribed entablature (fig.55). Clearly the capital originally supported it. The capital has a height of 0.93 metres, which is the same as that of the column-capital in Barcelona (fig.111). The Barcelona capital is an obvious candidate for the exedra columns, and it may safely be assumed that palm-tree pier-capitals stood at the corners of the exedrae, beneath the corner-blocks, whose measurements correspond.

The two piers in Venice and their capitals (fig.122), and the similar capital found in the excavation (fig.114), are about 20 per cent narrower. That they, too, belong to the lower storey is probable but not certain. The basket-capitals are smaller still. The split palmette capital (fig.108) and the lattice-capital (fig.110) are 0.695 and 0.59 metres high respectively, and can confidently be ascribed to an upper level. The cross-and-shell cornice (fig.106) also belongs to an upper storey, as is proved by its occurrence in the brick-pier from the western end of the church which had fallen into the atrium (fig.50).

The larger piers and their capitals were some 5 or 6 metres in height. Given the intervening inscribed entablature and a cornice, the gallery-floor can hardly have been less than 8 metres above the floor of the nave. The galleries, including (presumably) semi-domes over the exedrae, would have reduplicated this. Allowing a height (radius) of 9 metres for the four great arches, we may say that, if there was a dome, its seating would have been at least 25 metres above the nave-pavement and, if it was hemispherical, its crown would have been some 9 metres higher.

Internal furnishings included an ambo, inferred from the location and elliptical form of the foundation, and a ciborium over the altar, assumed from inlaid columns of appropriate size found in the area of the chancel (figs.54, 82, 83, 94). For the chancel-barrier, a structure presumably of plinths, posts and screens, perhaps with colonnettes, entablature, and even marble icons, there are abundant eligible fragments, none of which is conclusive. They include plinths of *antico verde*, posts of alabaster, and screens of Docimian marble. Most of these fragments are of Proconnesian marble.

Floors are presumed to have been paved with marble slabs, except perhaps in the nave where there was some evidence for geometric mosaic. Skirtings were of Proconnesian marble, and wall surfaces were clad with panels of coloured marble and elaborate inlays of amethyst, mother-of-pearl, coloured glass and shaped pieces of marble. In the apse, tall panels of carved marble were set between the windows (fig.134). The curved surfaces of vaults were covered with mosaic, mainly geometric but including some figures.

*170. Pier-capital with central date-palm.*

The principal approach to the church would have been by the atrium, where a broad staircase on the axis of the church gave access to the narthex, the floor of which was some 5 metres above that of the atrium. There would have been a direct approach, presumably at *piano nobile* (upper floor) level, from the palace. Some evidence was found for an external staircase or ramp at the northern end of the narthex, which would have given access to the gallery. It is not known whether there was a corresponding staircase at the south end of the narthex, or whether there were other staircases above, for example, the group of chambers in the northeast and south-east corners of the church. The atrium was planned to be half the width of the church and half (or more) as long again as its own width. On the north side it was overlooked by an elevated terrace, on which stood the square apsidal building which seems to have been a baptistery. No traces were found either of a corresponding building on the south side of the atrium, or of a range (including a gateway) across the western end.

With hindsight, neither the methods of construction nor the general form of the church of St. Polyeuktos were at all surprising. What was indeed remarkable was the decorative programme, both in its exuberance and variety; and the dimensions were quite astonishing.

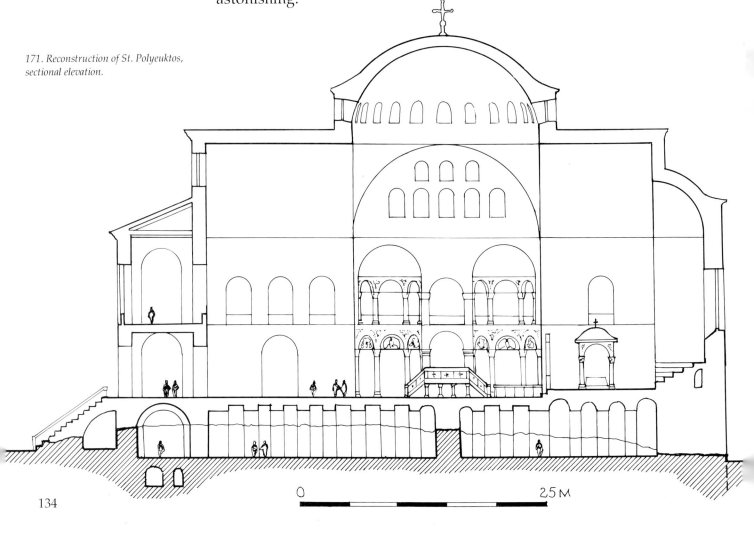

171. *Reconstruction of St. Polyeuktos, sectional elevation.*

0          25 M

172. *General view of north-west
complex of St. Polyeuktos, as excavated,
with possible location of Baptistery
(see Plan, fig. 48, for orientation).*

*173. Anicia Juliana, seated between personifications of Magnanimity and Prudence. Dedication miniature from the Vienna Dioscorides, a magnificent medical manuscript probably written about 512 A.D.*
*Vienna, Nationalbibliothek, Cod. Vind. Med. gr.1, folio 6 verso.*

# V · Conclusion:
# A New Temple of Solomon?

A CHURCH ON THE SCALE OF ST. POLYEUKTOS must have been built with a significant purpose. This grand gesture on the part of Anicia Juliana was clear in general political terms, for, as we have seen, her relations with the Emperor Justin were strained. Her aspirations are manifest in the poem, which stresses her royal ancestry and the continuity of her dynasty, but only now with these excavations have they become apparent in concrete form.

The recent discoveries reveal that the church had been laid out with accuracy and constructed with great care; yet the unit of measurement employed in its lay-out for a long time eluded us. Various kinds of 'foot' were tried, without success. It was not until 1982 that we realized that the unit had been the cubit and, more specifically, the royal cubit.[37] It was that discovery which explained the reference in the poem to Solomon's Temple, for Anicia Juliana clearly intended not only to vie with Solomon in all his kingly glory, but also to match the splendour of his building.

The cubit (traditionally the length of a man's forearm from the elbow to the clenched fist) is the principal unit of linear measurement in the Bible; it was also used in Egypt and in Mesopotamia.[38] It was incorporated into the later Greek and Roman systems of measurement, of which the basic unit was the foot, and it was still occasionally in use in Early Byzantine Constantinople.[39] There were, moreover, two kinds of unit; the standard measure of six hand-breadths, and the longer (or 'royal') cubit of seven. It has been computed that the common unit measured about 0.445 metres, the longer cubit about 0.518 metres. The church was 51.45 metres long and 51.90 metres broad which, with some allowance for error or subsidence, may be regarded as precisely one hundred 'long' or 'royal' cubits square. As the standard cubit was known in Constantinople, it would have been a simple calculation to determine the length of the long cubit.

This remarkable conjunction of dimensions provides a valuable clue to the intentions of the Byzantine princess, for the Temple at Jerusalem had been built in the tenth century B.C. as an expression of the kingship of Solomon in all his glory. It was a building of extraordinary splendour, and lengthy descriptions read like an architect's specifications for one of the Wonders of the World. (See I Kings, chapters 6 and 7, and II Chronicles, chapters 3 and 4; compare also the Heavenly Temple of Ezekiel, chapters 40-43.) The Temple was destroyed by Nebuchadnezzar in the sixth century B.C., rebuilt later in the same century, extensively reconstructed and adorned by Herod the Great in the first century B.C., and finally destroyed by the Romans in A.D. 70. But its fame survived, and Solomon and the Temple became for the Middle Ages symbols of divine kingship and royal (and indeed, heavenly) opulence. Besides, everybody knew the detailed description in the Book of Kings which represented Solomon's Temple and Palace as a model of royal building activity. As a further parallel to the Temple of Solomon, the church of Anicia Juliana was also the annexe to a palace.

The poem inscribed in the church claimed that Anicia Juliana 'alone had conquered time and surpassed the wisdom of the celebrated Solomon, raising a temple to receive God.' This may have been no idle boast, for the royal or long cubit is expressly mentioned by Ezekiel (40, 5: '... reckoning by the long cubit which was one cubit and a hand's breadth'), and his Temple was one hundred cubits long and, including the platform upon which it stood, one hundred cubits wide (41, 13-14: 'It was a hundred cubits long; and the free space, the building, and its walls, a hundred cubits in all. The eastern part of the temple and the free space was a hundred cubits wide'). Certain other measurements can be expressed in long cubits: the north wall of the atrium is just 75 cubits long (39.0m), the apsidal building (baptistery?) north of the atrium is 40 cubits square (20.80 metres), and the crypt of St. Polyeuktos is just under 20 cubits square (10.0 x 10.20 metres). If the crypt lay below a sanctuary which was, by an offset at floor-level in the walls, slightly larger, the sanctuary may have been exactly 20 cubits square, the precise dimensions of the Holy of Holies in the Temple of Solomon.

Coincidence of measurement is corroborated by coincidence of decoration. The Temple included palm-trees alternating with pairs of cherubim around the interior, open flowers, pomegranates, capitals overlaid with network, capitals in the form of lilies and, in the Herodian Temple, grapevines. 'Round all the walls of the house he carved figures of cherubim, palm-trees, and open flowers' (I Kings 6, 29) and '... cherubim and palm-trees, a pair between each pair of cherubim' (Ezekiel 41, 18). 'He made two bands of ornamental network, in festoons, of chain-work, for the capitals on the top of the pillars, a band of network for each capital. Then he made pomegranates in two rows all round on top of the ornamental network of the one pillar; he did the same with the other capital. The capitals at the top of the pillars in the vestibule were shaped like lilies ...' (I Kings 7, 17-19). 'A golden vine stood over the entrance to the Sanctuary' (*Middoth* 'Measurements', I, 4, 8).[40] These motifs, if we allow that the split-palmette capital resembles a lily (and John Ruskin in the nineteenth century noted that its nickname in Venice was 'capitello del giglio'), all recur in the exuberant decoration of the church of St. Polyeuktos (cf. figs.103, 110, 114, 120, 124), except perhaps the cherubim, whose form was never very explicit. The Jewish historian Josephus, speaking of the cherubim in the Temple, says that none could tell or even guess what they were like.[41] In interesting contrast to the Temple which had cherubim but no peacocks, the church had peacocks but no cherubim. Cherubim were zoomorphic, with wings and many eyes, and connoted royalty - and the same might be said to be true of peacocks, which were the birds of Empresses. In the circumstances it seems probable that the peacock, with its royal associations, was chosen to play this symbolic role in Anicia Juliana's programme.

The conclusion that Anicia Juliana was attempting to evoke the Temple is hard to resist. Her motive would have been to demonstrate her royal pretensions: for Solomon was the most kingly of kings and he had been crowned by Zadok the priest. This conceit was aimed at Justin who died, however, before the church was completed; but its meaning would not have been lost upon his successor.

St. Polyeuktos now stood as the largest and most sumptuous church in Constantinople, and thus Justinian's St. Sophia, in its scale, design and comparative austerity, is best seen as a deliberate reaction to it. St. Sophia was half as large again as St. Polyeuktos, with a dome one hundred Byzantine feet in diameter. The support of the dome by great semi-domes, themselves supported by open columnar exedrae, was an extraordinarily bold and elegant solution. Yet inside, the sculpture is far more restrained than that of St. Polyeuktos, in quantity, variety and design. It is principally used for the capitals, the arched entablatures of the two nave colonnades and four exedrae, and the cornices. The capitals are of the basket-type, with vestigial ionic volutes, completely overspun with a tracery of deeply undercut and etched acanthus leaves (fig.15). The entablatures also show an overall regular pattern of carefully undercut stylized acanthus scroll. The cornices, on the other hand,

174. A basket-capital from the main order of the church of San Vitale in Ravenna (between 526 and 546, but probably in the early part of the period). It is suggested that these split-palmette capitals were carved by sculptors who had worked on the church of St. Polyeuktos. Compare with Figs. 108 and 125.

175. Capital from Ayvan Saray in Istanbul and now in the Istanbul Archaeological Museum. (Max. width 0.70 metres.) Technically and stylistically this is closely related to th sculpture of St. Polyeuktos, and it is thought to be a product of the same workshop.

with their erect acanthus-leaves, acanthus-scroll, egg-and-dart and bead-and-reel decoration, show no advance on those of the early and mid fifth century.

Anicia Juliana's team of sculptors was large, expert and often hard-pressed. They operated mainly in the third year of the commission to complete the whole of the main entablature with the inscription as well as the capitals, cornices, piers and friezes. What became of the masons and sculptors on completion of the church? Some would have gone on to work on the church of St. Sergius and St. Bacchus, but this was a smaller and more modest project. Although it has fine basket-capitals and an inscribed frieze, the entablature, with its modillion-cornice, acanthus and traditional mouldings, is also reminiscent of fifth-century work (fig.16). Other craftsmen from the St. Polyeuktos workshop must have undertaken new commissions, for evidence of their work has come to light in a number of finds in the city including, for example, a pair of capitals from Ayvan Sarayi now in the Archaeological Museum (fig.175). What the facts seem to indicate, however, is that the team was not taken over *in toto* by Justinian, although the capital in Barcelona (fig.111) with its symmetrical design of horizontally splayed acanthus does suggest that at least some sculptors from St. Polyeuktos may have moved on to St. Sophia. If the whole work-force did not stay on to work for Justinian, what became of it?

176. Capital in the Basilica of
Euphrasius at Porec (Parenzo) in
Yugoslavia.

Part of the team appears to have travelled to Ravenna where the
church of San Vitale has in its main order fourteen capitals which
are of Proconnesian marble and strikingly similar to the split-
palmette capitals of St. Polyeuktos (fig.174). San Vitale was begun
by Ecclesius, Bishop of Ravenna from 521-531, who is represented
as Founder in the mosaic which decorates the apse. Although the
church was not completed until 547, the columns and capitals of
the main order are likely to belong to an early stage in the construction. It seems highly probable, too, that these capitals, like those at
St. Polyeuktos, would have been despatched in roughed-out state
to be completed on site, in line with normal practice. It is recorded
that Ecclesius visited Constantinople in 526,[42] which is precisely
the year in which Anicia Juliana's sculptors would have been hard
at work; it is tempting to suggest that he may have been shown the
church under construction and discussed there the possibility of a
commission at Ravenna to follow that of St. Polyeuktos.

That a group of sculptors migrated to the Adriatic is further
suggested by two capitals now in the Archiepiscopal Museum at
Ravenna, certain capitals in the Basilica of Euphrasius at Porec
(fig.176), and capitals in the Archaeological Museum at Split, from
a baptistery at Salona.[43] All are characterized by big-breasted birds
at the corners, which are carved in a style very similar to that of
the St. Polyeuktos peacocks (fig.91), and all have other features
which relate them to St. Polyeuktos. Until 540, when it fell to the
armies of Justinian, Ravenna had for half a century been the capital

141

of the Ostrogoths, a Germanic tribe which under their leader Theodoric captured the city in 493: both Porec and Salona lay within the Ostrogothic kingdom. Other elaborate sculpture, particularly in the Balkans and Asia Minor, suggests that the Constantinopolitan work-force may have split up and gone in different directions.

In 532, four or five years after Anicia Juliana's death, her son Flavius Anicius Olybrius was implicated in a plot against the Emperor and exiled.[44] His property, which presumably included the palace and its church, was confiscated. Although he was eventually permitted to return to Constantinople and his property was restored to him, he himself had no sons, and nothing is known of subsequent occupants of the palace or of the church's administration. The church could, however, still be visited in the tenth century. According to a recently published documentary source,[45] the relic of the head of St. Polyeuktos was apparently still there in the eleventh century. From the evidence of our own excavations it appears that the structure did not collapse before the end of the twelfth century. Moreover, apart from the early blocking of the passage beneath the nave, there is no evidence that the church was at any time modified, repaired or redecorated, and the impression is that it may have gone out of regular use at an early stage.

*177. Body of a peacock found in the excavations in Topkapi Saray in Istanbul in 1916 and now in the Istanbul Archaeological Museum. (Length 0.41 metres.) This corresponds exactly with the peacocks of St. Polyeuktos, from which it presumably originally came.*

By the fourteenth century (and presumably no earlier than the twelfth) the head of St. Polyeuktos had been transferred to the church of the Holy Apostles nearby.[46] We have seen that sculpture from the church of St. Polyeuktos has been found in the church of the Pantocrator (Zeyrek Camii) (fig.126) and in the Church of St. Andrew in Krisei (Koca Mustafa Pasa Camii) (fig.119). Elsewhere in the city a pier-capital has been found near Edirnekapi (fig.117), and a small fragment of vine-scroll has also been recognized in the monastery of Constantine Lips (Fenari Isa Camii).[47] A marble peacock excavated in Topkapi Sarayi is certainly from St. Polyeuktos (fig.177),[48] and a split-palmette capital at present exhibited in the garden of St. Sophia is probably from there as well (fig.178).[49] And although we do not know in what manner various marble piers and capitals were transferred to Venice, we do know however that this must have been in or soon after 1204, that is, after the Fourth Crusade. Three column-capitals were used to adorn the northern and southern ends of San Marco's western façade, and two piers, the so-called *pilastri acritani*, were erected in the Piazzetta, outside the south door of the Basilica.

Was there a parallel between San Marco and the Temple of Solomon, and also between the Doge's palace and the palace of Solomon?[50] Outside the main entrance of Solomon's Temple had stood two prominent piers called Jachin and Boaz, which were wrought by Hiram of Tyre (I Kings 7, 13-22). Perhaps the Venetians even believed that they had acquired Jachin and Boaz, or replicas of them, when they obtained the *pilastri acritani*?

What is now certain is that the remarkable sculpture of the ruined sixth-century church of St. Polyeuktos aroused keen interest during the thirteenth century. Fragments from the building have been identified, as we have seen, not only on several sites in Istanbul and in Venice, but also in Barcelona. It is probable that many more pieces will in the future be recognized and added to this ebullient repertory.[51]

As for the fate of the site of Anicia Juliana's church after 1204, it is clear, from the stratigraphy and from pottery and coins, that the ruins were quarried for marble and brick during the first half of the thirteenth century and again, after the Turkish Conquest in 1453, in the second half of the fifteenth century. For the two intervening centuries the site seems to have been deserted as, indeed, many of the large areas of the city were at this period, judging from historical sources.

*178. Fragmentary basket-capital of split-palmette type, in the garden of St. Sophia. It is probable that this originally came from St. Polyeuktos.*

In the last years of the fifteenth century the site, which had now been completely levelled, was reoccupied. Large houses were constructed on the northern part, and a mosque (the Karagöz Camii) on the southern part. Of the houses, which would have been of timber, only the shallow concrete foundations and, in one case, the foundations of a small bath-house, survived; but the status of the new residents and something of their life-style was clearly shown by the abundant contents of their rubbish-pits. These included not only fine Iznik pottery but imports of Italian maiolica and Chinese celadon, as well as ordinary household pottery and the discarded bones and shells from many meat and shellfish meals. Occupation seems to have been continuous until the present century, and the excavations have provided an extremely important pottery sequence for the whole of the Ottoman period. The mosque, for which documentary evidence also exists, was more substantially built, to judge from foundations found in the western part of the nave of St. Polyeuktos (fig.58). It was demolished about 1940, at the time of the construction of a major new north-south street, the Atatürk Bulvari. It seems likely that the area we excavated was first laid out as a public park at that time; our records include recent tree-pits beneath the paths of the new park which was created in 1960. That was the year when bulldozers uncovered accidentally those first marble fragments of Anicia Juliana's great church. The subsequent recovery, through six campaigns, of spectacular carvings and mosaics and structural remains made possible this amazing reconstruction of a grand Byzantine church, emulating the Temple of Solomon in conception and execution. Like the Temple of Jerusalem, the Church in Constantinople was part of a Palace and that Palace remains to be excavated. Now that the story of the Princess Anicia Juliana and her ambitions has been partly unfolded and in a way come full circle, surely more remains to be discovered and told.

# Notes

1. Notitia Urbis Constantinopolitanae, in, ed. O. Seeck, *Notitia Dignitatum* (1876; repr. Frankfurt am Main, 1962).

2. W. Müller-Wiener, *Bildlexikon zur Topographie Istanbuls* (Tübingen, 1977).

3. Theophanes, *Chronographia*, A.M. 6051 (ed. de Boor, pp.232-233).

4. Procopius, *De aedificiis* I, iv, 9-24 (Holy Apostles), and V, i, 4-6 (St. John).

5. J.B. Ward-Perkins, 'The Shrine of St. Menas in the Maryût', *Papers of the British School at Rome* 17 (1949), pp.26-71.

6. C. Mango, 'Isaurian Builders', in (ed. P. Wirth) *Polychronion. Festschrift Franz Dölger* (1966), pp.358-365; cf. also M. Gough, 'The Emperor Zeno and some Cilician churches', *Anatolian Studies* 22 (1972), pp.199-212.

7. R.M. Harrison, 'Churches and Chapels of Central Lycia', *Anatolian Studies* 13 (1963), pp.117-151.

8. J.B. Ward-Perkins, 'Building methods of Early Byzantine Architecture', in (ed. D. Talbot-Rice) *The Great Palace of the Byzantine Emperors* 2 (1958), pp.58-104.

9. The poem is *Greek Anthology* I, 10. The identification, which was first reported in *Byzantion* 29-30 (1959-1960), p.386 (cf. also pp.358-360), was fully discussed in C. Mango and I. Sevcenko, 'Remains of the church of St. Polyeuktos at Constantinople', *Dumbarton Oaks Papers* 15 (1961), pp.243-247.

10. *Codex Vindobonensis Med. Gr.* 1 of the Österreichische Nationalbibliothek; facsimile published with commentary by H. Gerstinger (Graz, 1970).

11. E. Alföldi-Rosenbaum, 'Portrait Bust of a Young Lady of the Time of Justinian', - *Metropolitan Museum Journal* 1 (1968), 19-40; K. Weitzmann (ed.), *Age of Spirituality. Late Antique and Early Christian Art, Third to Seventh Century* (New York, 1979), pp.292-295 (no.272).

12. For Anicia Juliana, see J.R. Martindale, *The Prosopography of the Later Roman Empire*, Vol.2 (1980), pp.635-6 and 1309; also C. Capizzi, 'Anicia Giuliana (462 ca - 530 ca): Ricerche sulla sua Famiglia e la sua Vita', *Rivista di Studi Bizantini e Neoellenici* 5 (15), 1968, pp.191-226.

13. *Patria* III, 57 (*Scriptores Originum Constantinopolitanarum*, ed. Th. Preger, p.237).

14. Gregory of Tours, *De gloria martyrum* (*Patrologia Latina* 71), cols.793-95.

15. For annual reports charting the progress of the excavation, see R.M. Harrison and N. Firatli, 'Excavations at Saraçhane in Istanbul', *Dumbarton Oaks Papers* 19 (1965), pp.230-236; 20 (1966), pp.233-238; 21 (1967), pp.273-278; 22 (1968), pp.195-203. Reports also appeared in *Türk Arkeoloji Dergisi* and *Istanbul Arkeoloji Müzeleri Yilligi*.

16. *De Caerimoniis* (ed. A. Vogt, pp. 68 and 43-4; ed. Reiske, pp. 75-6 and 50): from the account of the imperial procession for Easter Mondays.

17. Heidelberg, University Library, Cod. Pal. Gr.23.

18. For a general study of the materials, R. Gnoli, *Marmora Romana* (Rome, 1971).

19. J.B. Ward-Perkins, 'Quarrying in Antiquity. Technology, tradition, and social change', *Proceedings of the British Academy* 57 (1971), pp.3-24; *id.*, 'Nicomedia and the Marble Trade', *Papers of the British School at Rome* 48 (1980), pp.23-69; N. Asgari, 'Roman and Early Byzantine marble quarries of Proconnesus', *Proceedings of the Xth International Congress of Classical Archaeology, Ankara-Izmir 1973* (Ankara, 1978), pp.467-480.

20. F.W. Deichmann, *Ravenna* II, 2 (1976), pp.106-112, discusses the fourteen examples of this type in S.Vitale and gives a full list of those known from elsewhere.

21. R.M. Harrison, 'A Constantinopolitan capital in Barcelona', *Dumbarton Oaks Papers* 27 (1973), 297-300.

22. R.M. Harrison and N. Firatli, 'Excavations at Saraçhane in Istanbul: First Preliminary Report', *Dumbarton Oaks Papers* 19 (1965), p.234. R.M. Harrison, 'The Church of St. Polyeuktos in Constantinople', *Akten des VII Internationalen Kongresses für Christliche Archäologie, Trier 1965* (Vatican and Berlin, 1969), pp. 543-549. F. Deichmann, 'I Pilastri Acritani', *Rendiconti Atti della Pontificia Accademia Romana di Archeologia*, L (1980), pp. 75-89.

23. N. Asgari, 'Edirnekapi Basligi', *Arkeoloji ve Sanat* I, 2 (1978), pp.14-17.

24. The identification was made by Dr. Firatli.

25. R.M. Harrison, 'Anicia Juliana's church of St. Polyeuktos', *Jahrbuch der Österreichischen Byzantinistik* 32/4 (1982), pp.436-7.

26. A.H.S. Megaw, 'Notes on Recent Work of the Byzantine Institute in Istanbul', *Dumbarton Oaks Papers* 17 (1963), p.346 and fig.9.

27. R.M. Harrison and N. Firatli, 'Excavations at Saraçhane in Istanbul. Fourth Preliminary Report', *Dumbarton Oaks Papers* 21 (1967), p.276 and fig.12.

28. R.M. Harrison, 'Anicia Juliana's church of St. Polyeuktos', *Jahrbuch der Österreichischen Byzantinistik* 32/4 (1982), pp.437-8.

29. Persepolis: E. v. Mercklin, *Antike Figural Kapitelle* (Berlin, 1962), no.83; Hatra: J.B. Ward-Perkins, 'The Roman West and the Parthian East', *Proceedings of the British Academy* 51 (1965), p.192 and pl.LVb; Baalbek: *ibid*, p.191, pl.LVIIIa.

30. J.-P. Lauer and C. Picard, *Les statues ptolemaïques du Serapeion de Memphis* (Paris, 1955), pp.194-209, figs.98, 100-103, pls.19,20.

31. A. Grabar, 'Le rayonnement de l'art sassanide dans le monde chretien', *Accademia Nazionale dei Lincei, Quaderno* 160 (1971), pp.679-707 (esp.686-8); id., *Sculptures byzantines de Constantinople* (Paris, 1963), pp.64-65;

R.M. Harrison, 'The sculptural decoration of the church of St. Polyeuktos', *Actas del VIII Congreso Internacional de Arqueologia Cristiana, Barcelona 1969* (Vatican, Barcelona, 1972), pp.325-6.

32. C. Mango, 'Storia dell 'Arte', in *La civiltà bizantina dal IV al IX secolo* (Bari, 1977), pp.285-350.

33. K.A.C. Creswell, *Early Muslim Architecture* I, 1 (second ed., Oxford, 1969), pls.21c,26c,f; also, M.S. Dimand, 'Studies in Islamic Ornament. I. Some Aspects of Omaiyad and early Abbasid Ornament', *Ars Islamica* 4 (1937), pp.293-337, for a general discussion of the whole topic.

34. H. Luschey, 'Zur Datierung der Sassanidischen Kapitelle aus Bisutun und des Monuments von Taq-i-Bostan', *Teheraner Mitteilungen* 1 (1968), pp.129-142, esp. pl.52,6.

35. For Kish, A.U. Pope, *A Survey of Persian Art* 1 (London and New York, 1938), fig.168b; for an Assyrian example of the tree with streams of water, H. Frankfurt, *The Art and Architecture of the Ancient Orient* (2nd revised impression, Harmondsworth, 1958), pl.90.

36. This seems to be the earliest use of the basket-capital.

37. R.M. Harrison, 'The church of St. Polyeuktos in Istanbul and the Temple of Solomon', *Okeanos. Studies presented to Ihor Sevcenko* (*Harvard Ukrainian Studies* 7 (1983), pp.276-279. I owe the suggestion of the long cubit and its possible biblical connections to Mr. Michael Vickers.

38. R.B.Y. Scott, 'Weights and Measures of the Bible', *Biblical Archaeologist* 22, no.2 (1959), pp.22-41; id, 'The Hebrew Cubit', *Journal of Biblical Literature* 77, no.3 (1958), pp.205-214, and 'Postscript on the Cubit', *Journal of Biblical Literature* 79, no.4 (1960), p.368. I am grateful to Professor John Sawyer for help on this and following biblical matters.

39. Anonymus Byzantinus in (ed. H. Kochly and W. Rustow), *Griechische Kriegschriftstellen* II ii (1853-55), XII 1; also *Narratio de S. Sophiae*, 8-9 (transl. C. Mango, *The Art of the Byzantine Empire 312-1453* (Englewood Cliffs, N.J., 1972) ), p.97.

40. H. Danby, *The Mishnah* (Oxford, 1933; reprinted 1954), pp.589-598. This describes Herod's Temples, whose overall dimensions were also 100 cubits.

41. *Antiquitates Iudiacae* VIII, iii, 3.

42. A.A. Vasiliev, *Justin the First* (Cambridge, Mass., 1950), p.214.

43. Archiepiscopal Museum: R.O. Farioli, *La scultura architettonica* (Rome, 1969), nos.50,51; Porec: C. Mango, *Byzantine Architecture* (New York, 1976), pl.70; Archaeological Museum, Split: J.J. Wilkes, *Dalmatia* (London, 1969), pl.56.

44. Malalas, *Chronographia* XVIII (Bonn ed., in *Patrologia Graeca* 97), p.478, 11, 18-21.

45. K.N. Ciggaar, 'Une description de Constantinople traduite par un pèlerin anglais', *Revue des Études Byzantines* 34 (1976), pp.211-267.

46. B. de Khitrowo, *Itinéraires russes en Orient* (Geneve, 1889), pp.104,137,162,203; cf. R. Janin, *Les églises et les monastères* (Paris, 1953), pp.419-20.

47. C. Mango, E.J.W. Hawkins, 'Additional finds at Fenari Isa Camii', *Dumbarton Oaks Papers* 22 (1968), p.178, fig.9.

48. J. Ebersolt, *Mission archéologique de Constantinople* (Paris, 1921), 4 and pl.XXIV, 3.

49. U. Peschlow, 'Dekorative Plastik aus Konstantinopel an San Marco in Venedig', *Apherioma stê mnêmê Stylianou Pelekanidê.* (Thessaloniki, 1983), pp.406-417 and pl.2c,d.

50. D. Rosand, *Painting in Cinquecento Venice* (Yale University Press, 1983), p. 127: 'The Palace of the Doges ... was itself deliberately associated with the Palace of Solomon.' I am grateful to Mr M. Vickers for this information.

51. A start has been made in Venice by the work of U. Peschlow, *loc. cit.* (note 49).

# Further Reading

A. Grabar, *Sculptures Byzantines de Constantinople (IVe-Xe siècle)* (Paris, 1963).

R. M. Harrison, *Excavations at Saraçhane in Istanbul*, Vol. I, (Princeton University Press and Dumbarton Oaks, 1986).

R. Krautheimer, *Early Christian and Byzantine Architecture* (4th edition with S. Curcic, reprinted Harmondsworth, 1988).

C. Mango, *Byzantine Architecture* (New York, 1975).

C. Mango 'Storia dell' Arte', in *La civiltà bizantina dal IV al IX secolo* (Bari, 1977), pp. 285-350.

T.F. Mathews, *The Early Churches of Constantinople. Architecture and Liturgy* (University Park, Pa., London, 1971).

T.F. Mathews, *The Byzantine Churches of Istanbul. A Photographic Survey* (University Park, Pa., London, 1976).

W. Müller-Wiener, *Bildlexikon zur Topographie Istanbuls* (Tübingen, 1977).

C. Strube, *Polyeuktoskirche und Hagia Sophia: Umbildung und auflösung antiker Formen, Entstehen des Kämpferkapitells.* (Munich, 1984).

J. B. Ward-Perkins, 'Notes on the Structure and Building Methods of Early Byzantine Architecture', in *The Great Palace of the Byzantine Emperors. Second Report* ed. D. Talbot (Edinburgh Univ. Press, 1958).

# CHRONOLOGY

| Century | Emperors | Events | Buildings in Constantinople |
|---|---|---|---|
| **300** | Diocletian (284-305) | | |
| | Constantine (306-337) | Constantine's capture of Rome (312) and adoption of Christianity | |
| | | Foundation of Constantinople (324-30) | Porphyry column (325/330) |
| | | | First St Sophia (ded. 360) |
| | | | Aqueduct of Valens (begun 368) |
| | Theodosius I (379-95) | | |
| | | Closure of Pagan Temples (390) | Golden Gate (?), Obelisk, Forum, Arch (c. 390) |
| **400** | | | |
| | | Capture of Rome by Goths (410) | Land Walls (413) |
| | | | Second St Sophia (ded. 415) |
| | Theodosius II (408-50) | | |
| | | | St John of Studios (c. 450) |
| | | Deposition of last Emperor of Roman West (476) | |
| | Zeno (474-91) | | |
| | | Capture of Italy and Ravenna by Ostrogoths (493) | |
| **500** | | | |
| | Anastasius (491-518) | | |
| | Justin I (527-65) | S. Vitale, Ravenna, begun (526?) | St Polyeuktos (524-27) Sts Sergius and Bacchus (after 527) |
| | | Byzantine expeditionary forces to recover Africa, Italy and Spain (533-555) | Third St Sophia (532-537 |
| | | Byzantine recapture of Ravenna (540) | |
| | | Dedication of S. Vitale, Ravenna (546/47) | |
| | | | St Sophia dome rebuilt (558-62) |

# GENEALOGY

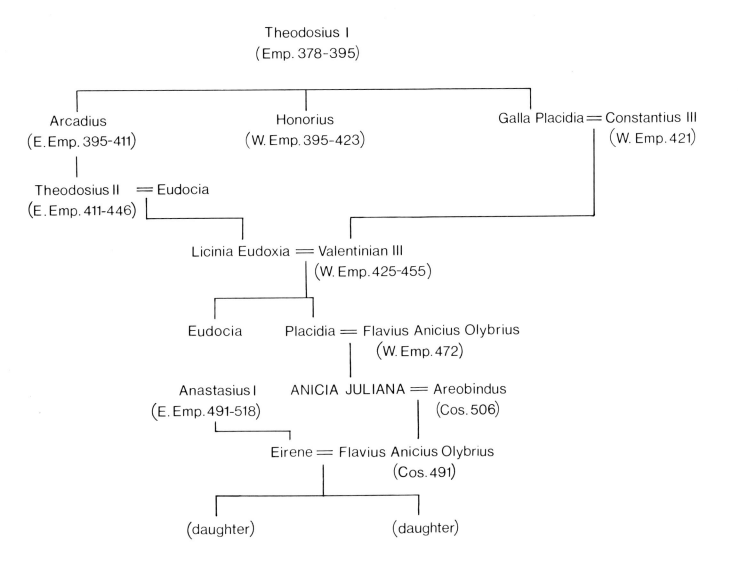

Theodosius I
(Emp. 378-395)

Arcadius
(E. Emp. 395-411)

Honorius
(W. Emp. 395-423)

Galla Placidia ═ Constantius III
(W. Emp. 421)

Theodosius II ═ Eudocia
(E. Emp. 411-446)

Licinia Eudoxia ═ Valentinian III
(W. Emp. 425-455)

Eudocia

Placidia ═ Flavius Anicius Olybrius
(W. Emp. 472)

Anastasius I
(E. Emp. 491-518)

ANICIA JULIANA ═ Areobindus
(Cos. 506)

Eirene ═ Flavius Anicius Olybrius
(Cos. 491)

(daughter)        (daughter)

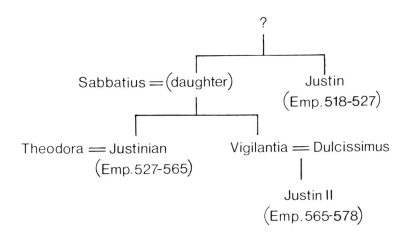

?

Sabbatius ═ (daughter)        Justin
(Emp. 518-527)

Theodora ═ Justinian        Vigilantia ═ Dulcissimus
(Emp. 527-565)

Justin II
(Emp. 565-578)

# Glossary of Architectural Terms

**Abacus**

A narrow rectangular block (usually square) which forms the topmost element of a capital

**Acanthus**

A plant with spiky leaves, often used in architectural ornament

**Ambo**

A pulpit, often elliptical in form

**Astragal**

Another word for the bead-and-reel (lit = knucklebone)

**Atrium**

A courtyard constituting the main approach to a church

**Baldacchino**

A free-standing canopy above an altar, throne or tomb

**Basket-capital**

A column-capital of near hemispherical shape, in the form of a basket

**Bead-and-reel**

A narrow moulding of semicircular profile, decorated with an alternating scheme of one long and two short beads (also called astragal, from the Greek for knucklebone)

**Cantharus**

A vase with foot, neck and two handles, often depicted with plants issuing from it

**Ciborium**

Canopy *see Baldacchino*

**Composite capital**

A kind of Corinthian capital with, instead of Corinthian volutes rising beneath each corner of the abacus, Ionic volutes placed horizontally between the bell and the abacus

**Corinthian capital**

A capital in the form of an inverted bell supporting a square abacus; acanthus-leaves grow up around the bell, and from them rise four volutes, one to support each corner of the abacus

**Corona**

The face of the projecting upper part of a cornice

**Cyma recta**

A moulding whose profile is S-shaped, with a convex above a concave curve, often decorated with a leaf-and-tongue

**Cyma reversa**

A moulding whose profile is S-shaped, with a concave above a convex curve, often decorated with erect acanthus leaves

**Egg-and-dart**

A narrow, quarter-round moulding decorated with an alternating egg and down-pointed dart (also called ovolo)

**Entablature**

The architrave, frieze, and (usually) cornice above supporting columns or piers

**Exedra**

A rectangular or curvilinear bay known, if it is defined by columns, as an open columnar exedra

**Fillet**

A narrow flat moulding

**Hood**

A projecting, cornice-like block placed above a lintel

**Leaf-and-tongue**

A series of pendant leaves each alternating with a narrow 'tongue', usually on a cyma recta moulding

**Modillion**

An approximately square panel set horizontally upon the underside of a projecting cornice

**Narthex**

The vestibule of a church, usually the full width of the church's façade

**Ovolo**

A quarter-round moulding, decorated with egg-and-dart

### Pendentive

In a square bay defined by four arches of equal diameter and height whose crowns touch the horizontal seating for a dome, the masonry between adjacent arches which rises to support that seating. The form is triangular, with three concave sides and concave curvature in both vertical and horizontal planes

### Protome

The forepart of an animal or bird carved in protuberant high relief

### Rebate

Step-shaped reduction cut along an edge or face

### Roundel

A narrow half-round moulding, often decorated with bead-and-reel (astragal)

### Squinch

A corbelling, usually a small arch, which is placed across the corners of a square bay to form an octagon suitable for an octagonal or domical roof

### Triconchos

A church (or other building) with apses (conches) on three sides of a square bay

# The Symbolism

### The Eagle

This represented Zeus in the Greek world and Jupiter in the Roman, and also the Roman Emperor, including his apotheosis and immortality; in Judaean and Christian periods the Eagle represented spiritual regeneration.

### The Peacock

This stood for Hera in the Greek world and Juno in the Roman, and, like the Eagle, it represented the Roman Empress, in particular for apotheosis and immortality; in Judaean and Christian art it stood for immortality, incorruptible flesh, and everlasting life.

### The Palm-tree

In the Greek and Roman periods, as well as the Judaean and Christian, the Palm-tree stood for fecundity and victory. It was graceful, with evergreen foliage, and delicious fruit.

### The Pomegranate

This, like the Palm-tree, also represented fecundity and victory, and, by its multitudinous seeds, showed the change from death to life.

### The Vine

This represented Dionysus (Bacchus) in the Greek and Roman periods, with its fecundity and life-giving force. In the Judaean and Christian periods it stood for prolific growth and immortality. Christ calls himself the True Vine.

# List of Illustrations

# Index

*Illustration numbers are shown in italic*

*Silver liturgical spoon found at St. Polyeuktos.*
*6th or possibly early 7th century.*